Naive Questions about War and Peace

WILLIAM WHITWORTH

CONVERSATIONS WITH EUGENE V. ROSTOW, former Under-Secretary of State for Political Affairs

W · W · NORTON & COMPANY · INC ·
NEW YORK

Copyright © 1970 by William Whitworth

Of the material in this book, a considerable portion originally appeared as an article in *The New Yorker* and was copyright © 1970 by The New Yorker Magazine, Inc.

FIRST EDITION

SBN   393   05430   6

Library of Congress Catalog Card No. 71-133611

Published simultaneously in Canada
by George J. McLeod Limited, Toronto

PRINTED IN THE UNITED STATES OF AMERICA

1 2 3 4 5 6 7 8 9 0

To Carolyn

✦✦✦✦✦✦✦✦✦✦✦✦✦✦✦✦✦✦✦✦✦✦✦✦✦✦✦✦✦✦✦✦✦✦✦✦✦✦✦

CONTENTS

*Naive Questions
about War and Peace*

++

ONE

The Balance of Power

Why are we in Vietnam? How is our security involved with that of Southeast Asia? And what do politicians and journalists mean by "national security" or "the national interest"? What do they mean by "balance of power"? Why do we want to "contain" China? As an ignorant layman trying to follow the course of the war in Vietnam, I've been tormented for years by such questions. It seems that the public discussion of the war has been conducted largely on two levels, and that discussion on a third level has been neglected. On the first level, critics of the war have raised the moral questions about it fully and eloquently. They have made us wonder, for example, whether we are not actually destroying a country that we claim to be protecting. On the second level of discussion, they have raised countless questions about the military and political nature of the war and of Southeast Asia, such as: Is this really a war of aggression, or is it a civil war? Would a victory by the Vietcong and the North Vietnamese mean an increase in Chinese power, or would it actually mean the establishment of a nation that, though Communist, would resist Chinese expansion? Did bombing of the North prolong or shorten the war? Would the other dominoes *necessarily* fall if South Vietnam did?

A strong case against the war was made long ago on these two levels, I think, but there are still many unanswered questions on a third one: that of the geopolitical thinking behind the war—the realm of foreign-policy premises so fundamental in our national life that they are shared by supporters of the war and many of its opponents, and thus are seldom discussed. One such fundamental premise is that the United States has some sort of vital interest in Asia. Doves and hawks who share this premise disagree about whether the war in Vietnam is furthering this unstated interest or hindering it. But for someone who doesn't share or understand this premise the question about the domino theory, for example, is not "Will the dominoes really fall?" but "From a selfish standpoint, why should we care if they *do* fall?" In other words, does the United States have any real national interest—strategic or economic, honorable or dishonorable—in Southeast Asia? Would the "loss" of Southeast Asia really change the international balance of power in a way that would endanger the United States? Our government has

12

acted for many years on the assumption that such a
change would endanger us. But, as far as I know, it
has never explained this assumption in any concrete
way, and the press has not demanded that it do so.

Once you question this assumption, other questions
follow: We had good reason for containing Russia's
expansion in Europe and preserving our economic and
cultural ties with Western Europe, but do we have a
similar interest in containing China in Asia? Is the war
in Vietnam based on a poor analogy with European
conflicts of the past? Why do American interests require "stability in Asia? What does "balance of power"
mean in the nuclear era? Doesn't power today consist
more of technological and economic strength than of
territorial control? Now that China has nuclear
weapons, how could geographical expansion increase
her threat to us? If China swallowed all of Asia and
Africa, would it make her stronger or weaker? If our
economic interest in Africa and Asia is slight, and if
the West's need for the raw materials of the underdeveloped countries is declining rather than increasing,
what does the United States care how much turmoil
China encourages in those areas or how much influence she wields? If we fear bombs, China already
has them; and if we fear the manpower of the Third
World, what concrete expression can that fear be
given? Would China drop Cambodians and Laotians
and Nigerians on us from airplanes? Send them to
our shores in thousands of tiny rowboats? Do we have

13

to contain China because we have a real conflict with her, or do we have a conflict with her because we think we have to contain her?

Perhaps, this late in our involvement in Southeast Asia, questions of this sort are academic, but I don't believe they are. We are still in Vietnam, and in the coming years we may be faced with other potential Vietnams. With this thought in mind, I decided recently to try to pose these balance-of-power questions to someone who had served in the Johnson Administratinn, who understood the war policy, and who still supported it. Though I opposed the war, I didn't want to discuss these questions with a critic of the war—it was the thinking of the Johnson Administration that I was interested in. My idea was that, in all the years of the debate, the Administration's spokesmen hadn't been forced to defend the war at the geopolitical level. (In Senator J. W. Fulbright's Senate Foreign Relations Committee hearings, for instance, Dean Rusk always managed to tie up the discussion at the level of, say, the United States' obligations under the SEATO treaty. The question of whether we should have gotten into the war in the first place was dealt with in generalities or was brushed aside as academic.) If they had a plausible defense, I thought it should be heard. If they couldn't make such a defense when faced with these fundamental questions, then this failure would provide opponents of the war with still another basis on which to oppose it. Neither did I want

14

to talk with any of Nixon's advisers, because they could argue that they had inherited the war and were now concerned only with how to get out of it without weakening the credibility of American commitments elsewhere in the world. President Johnson himself wasn't available for an interview. Dean Rusk said at first that he might talk with me and then, several days later, that he'd rather not. "There's no mystery about it, though," the former Secretary of State told me on the phone. "Four Presidents have concluded that if Southeast Asia, with all its people and resources, came under Communist control, it would be adverse to the interests of the United States." I said yes, I knew that, but I wondered just *how* it would be adverse, and what the components of the threat would be. "Well, these things don't break down, they're just broad concepts," Rusk said. Walt Rostow, who was a Special Assistant to President Johnson and is high on the war critics' list of Vietnam culprits, expressed mild sympathy for my project but declined to participate. William Bundy, who was also prominent among the Vietnam policymakers, as Assistant Secretary of State for Far Eastern Affairs, agreed with me that the questions I wanted to raise had been largely ignored in the press, and he seeemed interested in discussing them. "You wouldn't find me very combative on any of these matters," Bundy said. He, too, eventually declined to be interviewed, saying that medical problems required him to limit his activities for a while.

15

The only high-ranking member of the Johnson Administration I found who retains both his belief in the necessity of the war and his willingness to defend it in public was Walt Rostow's brother, Eugene V. Rostow, who was Johnson's Under-Secretary of State for Political Affairs—the third-ranking man in the Department—from 1966 to 1969. Eugene Rostow did not, as did his brother, share with President Johnson in the formation of American policy for Southeast Asia, but he is familiar with the thinking behind that policy, according to Rusk. A lawyer and economist, Rostow was dean of the Yale Law School from 1955 to 1965 and is now Sterling Professor of Law and Public Affairs there. His experience in foreign affairs, in addition to his term as Under-Secretary, includes service as an assistant to Dean Acheson from 1942 to 1944, when Acheson was Assistant Secretary of State; as an assistant, in 1949 and 1950, to Gunnar Myrdal, who was then executive secretary of the United Nations Economic Commission for Europe, in Geneva; and as a consultant to Under-Secretary of State George W. Ball from 1961 to 1966. In addition, he is a member of the Atlantic Council, and is the author of numerous articles and four books, including *Law, Power, and the Pursuit of Peace,* an explanation of American foreign policy since the Second World War.

When Rostow agreed to try to answer my questions about Foreign policy, I went to see him in New

16

Haven. I found him at work in the Law School, in an office comfortably furnished with a sofa, two easy chairs, a rocker, and an Oriental rug. He is a tall, slender, gray-haired man of fifty-six, and he is an urbane, pleasant host. We talked for about three hours that day, for an hour at a second meeting, and for two hours at a third. (The talks are presented here as a single discussion.) Our discussion was inconclusive, of course; Rostow felt afterward that he had swept away my basic objections to the policy he defended, and I was equally convinced that I had asked some questions that he could not answer satisfactorily. If the discussion seems not only inconclusive but narrow, that is because I restricted it to questions on what I have described as a third level; that is, to questions about the international balance of power—to the exclusion of moral questions and questions about such details of the war as bombing halts, peace negotiations, "pacification," treaty interpretations, and so on. I began by asking Rostow if he would try to explain to me how American security depended upon the security of Southeast Asia. He answered with a short history lecture.

"I believe that foreign policy should be addressed only to our safety as a nation—that there is no difference between a 'liberal' foreign policy and a 'conservative' foreign policy," Rostow said. "Our safety as a nation has always depended—and this was perceived early in the history of the Republic—on there being a balance of power in Europe and a balance of power in

17

Asia, so that no hegemonic power, no one power, would acquire so much strength in either place that it would be free of all restraints from rivals at home, and thus able to become a threat to the United States. Now, obviously, when we're dealing with the world of the Napoleonic era, when threats were measured in terms of the speed of sailing ships, that presented policymakers with one set of problems—that is, a concern about penetrations of this hemisphere, summed up in the idea of the Monroe Doctrine. The problem of security is totally different today, when we're dealing with nuclear threats in the first place and in the second place with threats from conventional military power based on enormously improved communications, transportation, and firepower. I think the essence of the American problem is that we lived for a century or more in the system of security that was organized by the European concert of nations which had been started after the Napoleonic Wars. That protected us without any effort on our part and really without any consciousness of the problem on our part. The result is that our national attitude toward foreign affairs is deeply rooted in the view that we are a republic and a democratic society and our safety simply depends on our own inherent virtues and not on the exertions of the British fleet or the balance of power in Europe or in Asia. We've always known in a way that that wasn't true, at the level of instinct. We had an instinct for self-preservation that led us into the First World War

18

despite our disinclination to go in. I think President Johnson said once that we went into the first war to protect an interest that most Americans weren't aware of or would have opposed if they were aware of it; namely, to preserve a balance of power in Europe, to prevent a potentially hostile Germany from dominating Europe. At that time, we had seen in connection with German activities in Mexico what implications German victory might have had for us close to home.

"Today, we live in a world in which three enormous flows of change are happening at once. First is the liquidation of empire, the withdrawal of the European states to Europe. The second is the rise of Communist powers, and I put that in the plural—their are different forms of Communisim, and they are dividing, but nonetheless they combine on certain occasions, and the Soviet Union has enormous nuclear strength and conventional strength. And the third is the rise of our own response. The consequence of the withdrawal of Europe from the world has been that the Balkan problem, which used to be a *Balkan* problem, is now almost universal. We have many nations in Africa and Asia which have been liberated from the control of empire but are weak and vulnerable, both from within and from without.

"Now, our response, starting after the Second World War, when we began to realize that our earnest and sustained efforts to reach an accommodation with the Soviet Union, to reach a pattern of coöperation with

19

them, based on economic aid and coöperation in eliminating the nuclear threat—when we realized that those efforts had failed, we set about to create a situation of stability in the world; really, to establish a new balance of power. The title of Dean Acheson's great book is *Present at the Creation*. And there is a deep truth in that title, because at the end of the war we faced a situation in which the world political system was in chaos. The system that had kept the peace more or less between 1815 and 1914 disintegrated between 1914 and 1945, and in 1945 it was finished. Russia, China, Japan—these were countries on a new scale, as far as European capacity was concerned, and the Europeans were engaged in a slow, painful withdrawal from their positions of empire, which had preserved a kind of stability in the world political system for a long time. We gradually became aware of a national interest in achieving a new balance of power, within which we could hope to live as a free society, a balance of power which could permit us to survive pretty much in terms of our historic patterns. I like to turn Wilson's remark around: Wilson talked about making the world safe for democracy—we need a world in which American democracy would be safe at home. I don't think we could survive as a democratic nation if we were alone and isolated in a world of hostility, chaos, and poverty. I think our instinct was right shortly after the war, when President Truman finally drew the line and said, 'Thus far, and no further,' about Iran, Greece, Turkey,

20

and Berlin, and later Korea. Now, our rhetoric, our way of talking about problems of national security, hasn't yet caught up with our instincts. We're aware of the fact that the world is much smaller, much more dangerous than it used to be, and that the powers that used to protect us can do so no longer. But we find it extremely difficult to realize that we have a permanent interest in protecting the independence and the territorial integrity of Western Europe, of Japan, and of many other parts of the world which are necessary to constitute a system of order. Many people say this policy is globalism, or it's an anti-Communist crusade. It's neither one. Let me take the second point first. Are we engaged in an anti-Communist crusade? The United States never dreamed of attacking the Soviet Union or of delivering an ultimatum to the Soviet Union at a time when we had the nuclear monopoly. Nor, indeed, did we undertake to change the arrangements which emerged in Eastern Europe, although these arrangements were contrary to agreements that had been made with us at both Yalta and Potsdam. These things happened, they alarmed us and concerned us, but we didn't think of using force to undo them. What happened was that we said, in effect, that the process of outward expansion by the Soviet Union is beginning to threaten the possibility of equilibrium in the world, and that the safest rule is the rule that President Truman laid down—'Thus far, and no further.'

"Now, most people, I think, understand and accept

21

that kind of balance-of-power reasoning about Europe and about Japan, because these are obviously enormous centers of power. And to add them to the Soviet or the Chinese list of resources could be potentially very dangerous, in term of old instincts about the balance of power. But why do we have to worry about smaller countries, which in themselves don't amount to much in terms of power? Why Korea? Why Vietnam? Why are we concerned about the Middle East? Well, to take the Middle East first—because that's a problem on which I worked hard and long in Washington—manifestly, the United States isn't threatened if Syria or another small country in the Middle East becomes, in effect, a Soviet satellite. There are, of course, implications for the problem of power if Soviet naval bases or airbases are established in Syria or Algeria. Such a dispersion of Soviet power would present problems for us in the nuclear field of targeting and deterrence. The issue is one of degree. In the Middle East, the Soviets are using Arab-Israeli hostility as an engine to stir up terrific political movements in the Arab world—political movements whose goal is to destroy the kind of moderate government that exists in Lebanon, in Tunisia, in Jordan, in Saudi Arabia, ultimately even in Iran. Complete Soviet control in the area, or nearly complete control, would be a genuine threat.

"If you look at this Soviet effort as a military campaign, what do you see? You see, in the first place, that Europe is outflanked. The military arrangements of NATO and of the Warsaw Pact powers in the middle of Europe, facing each other, deterring each other, become almost as irrelevant as the Maginot Line if Soviet power is extended all the way around to Algeria, Tunisia, Libya, and so on. And there are possibilities of explosions in the Middle East, involving Israel or other countries, which could bring us to the kind of panic, the kind of atmosphere of rage, which is the real cause of war. War comes when people feel that the moorings are slipping, when the situation is getting out of hand and there's a slide toward chaos which threatens their sense of safety. I can't imagine that Europe or the United States would stand by and see Israel destroyed, no matter *what* people think now. The actual event, if it began to happen, would precipitate an enormous revulsion, colored, of course, by the Nazi experience. Israel is a country that exists by virtue of a decision made by the United Nations, and by the United States and the Soviet Union, in 1947, and people have lived there, a community has been formed, and we're simply not going to stand by and see these people pushed into the sea.

"Now, this area involves a terrific risk, because arms are being poured into the Middle East, hostility is being mounted. You can say, 'Well, what is our interest there?' Well, our interest is in preventing a convulsion that could threaten the possibility of peace. It's an interest in the people, an interest in the integrity of

23

commitments, but above all it's an interest in the possibility of peace. And if the Soviet Union came to dominate and occupy the whole of the Middle East, we would be threatened strategically in a way that would touch psychological nerves and create the kind of risk we faced in the Cuban missile crisis. You can say, 'Well, why were we so excited by the Cuban missile crisis?' Yes, the Soviet Union had lied to President Kennedy about those missiles. Missiles in Cuba are very close to the United States. On the other hand, there are missiles on Soviet submarines. And missiles can reach the United States from the Soviet Union itself, and from bombers. But the Cuban episode is worth studying because *we were ready to go then.* There was a rage in the country and a sense of threat, and these were extremely dangerous. Was it rational or irrational? Now, I think that one of the main objectives of our foreign policy should be to prevent those risks from developing. Of course, the problem is infinitely more difficult throughout the Third World than it is in Europe or in Japan. Now let me come to Vietnam."

"Could I interrupt about what you just said?" I asked.

"Oh, sure."

"About Cuba. You seem to be saying that if we didn't look at things the way we do look at them, the risk really, physically, apart from some psychological reaction, was no greater to us during that crisis than it is all the time. As you say, there are Soviet submarines, and we can be struck by missiles from the Soviet Union."

"Well, this is the nature of the dual threat that we face in the modern world because of the existence of nuclear weapons," Rostow said. "At one level, there is the nuclear threat. We and the Soviets are major nuclear powers. In many ways, nuclear weaponry is a cancerous growth. It's a very difficult thing to think about rationally, but everybody I know, from one end of the spectrum to the other, agrees that in the face of Soviet nuclear developments we have to at least remain in a position of deterrence. And deterrence is a complicated thing that keeps changing as technology changes. What *about* the defensive weapons? What *about* new systems of submarine attack? And so on. But for ordinary life, one simply assumes a nuclear stalemate—that is, that one is living in a nearly non-nuclear world. And in the world of ordinary non-nuclear diplomacy the necessity for equilibrium, sustained by conventional means, remains what it always has been. The nuclear weapon can't and ought not to be used, save in the most unimaginable circumstances. Therefore, the struggle for peace must go on by ordinary means."

"But during the Cuban missile crisis," I said, "were we more threatened from a technological standpoint than we had been before the missiles were installed?"

"No. I think we were just touching a nerve of concern."

"We were not more threatened technologically?"

"Well, we may have been at that point," Rostow said. "But, in retrospect, the missile threats are now equal or greater. I've forgotten exactly where the Soviets stood then in terms of long-range or seaborne missiles. But the threat as of that moment exists now, the nuclear threat exists now. And, of course, there's also the political threat, the threat of subversion mounted from Cuba against South American countries, which is a nuisance. And many people think that we ought to eliminate Castro from Cuba. I don't agree. I don't think Castro is an insuperable threat. But the missile crisis was a situation that I think is important for us to think about, because we were ready to go. And Europe was ready to go."

"But wasn't it greatly because of, as you say, this psychology? And because you had a Republican senator—Keating, of New York—raising hell about it and putting pressure on the President, and the President not wanting to look as though he weren't doing his job?"

"That's part of it," Rostow said. "But, of course, you have to deal with psychological factors as well as more tangible ones."

"But if the government didn't help create this psychology, if it didn't promote this—"

"But you see, if you look at the background of the thing, Kennedy had seen Khrushchev in Vienna and had had a most unpleasant time. He had made an

26

agreement about Laos, which was a genuinely important agreement, and it wasn't being enforced. Probably a lot of the tragedy of Vietnam stems from that fact. He was given another challenge, in Cuba, and he reacted very strongly. If you look at the onset of wars, there is always a series of episodes—alarm clocks, Vansittart called them—which stir up what he called instincts of self-preservation."

"In a situation like that," I said, "do you fear the Russian reaction or the domestic reaction? Is it that the President might lose his office, or are you afraid that the form of government itself is in danger, that the generals might take over, or what?"

"No, it's not anything cynical, like the fear of losing office," Rostow said. "You go back to the phenomenon of war, and the decision to use force, not as a chess-game problem at all but as a very complex psychological phenomenon that involves fears, concerns, risks that sometimes can't be concretely identified. Now, as far as President Kennedy was concerned in the Cuban crisis —I wasn't involved, but I've talked a lot with some of the people who were—my reconstruction of it would be this: that Kennedy's perception of the fundamental political problem for the United States, the problem of security for the United States, was that our relationship with the Soviet Union was critical. He felt that the Russians would push him until they were deterred from pushing, that they were testing him and probing him, first in Vienna, then in Laos. The Bay of Pigs, he felt,

27

was an indication to them of weakness or uncertainty in his handling of our affairs. And he was at great pains to reëstablish the deterrent power of a firm American position, which was the basic force that had kept the general peace throughout the world ever since 1947. Now, the domestic political consequences were perfectly real in Kennedy's mind. In his campaign for the Presidency, he had pounded at the Republicans for allowing the Soviets to get established in Cuba. But I'm sure his dominant concern was the state of tension between the Soviet Union and the United States. All politics is a function of extremely complex variables, which have different weights. And foreign policy since the war and the disintegration of the old world system has become a form of politics which has to be played at many levels. It's almost impossible to anticipate all the levels. That's one of the many reasons the restoration of an understood and accepted system of minimal public order is so important. Because the risks of the present international system are so enormous. It's fundamentally a fragile system that hasn't yet jelled."

TWO

Vietnam and Japan

The conversation moved on to Vietnam, and Rostow recounted at some length the history of our involvement. The commitments that President Eisenhower made there were part of the process of ending the Korean war and the wave of hostilities in the Far East following the Second World War, he said. Eisenhower saw the fighting in Vietnam, Korea, and Malaysia as three fronts of the same expansionist effort. After a stalemate was achieved in Korea, we and the Russians both made efforts, at Geneva and elsewhere, to end the fighting in Indo-China. We made commitments in the SEATO agreement. From the point of view of international law, Rostow said, it didn't make any difference whether the war was an insurrection mounted within South Vietnam and supported by North Vietnam or a war mounted from North Vietnam. The agreements at Geneva had set up two entities, and

29

assisting an insurrection against a government was just as much an act of war, in international law, as attacking it directly. Whatever hope there was now of peaceful coexistence in the world depended upon Chinese and Russian respect for American commitments. We were currently trying to put together a system of peace. If an American commitment should be proved worthless, what effect would this have upon calculations by the Chinese, the Russians, the Japanese?

When he had finished, I said, "I can understand all that, in the context in which you're speaking, but I'm trying to get you to go back before some of those assumptions. As Richard J. Barnet said in *No More Vietnams*, we keep seeing Vietnam as another confrontation the Communists have arranged simply to test our nerve, as another test case. He described this as an egocentric view of the world, in which other nations exist only to provide sparring partners for us. The thing in Indo-China had been going on for a long time, in one form or another. What if the French hadn't been there? What if Eisenhower's view of the world was wrong? Maybe the Vietnamese don't see themselves as simply another front in some worldwide effort."

"Foy Kohler, who was one of my colleagues in Washington, used to say that the trouble with foreign-policy work is that you have to take the world as it is," Rostow said. "You can't go back and say we should have done something else twenty years ago. I don't mean to say there's no use talking about what happened then, or what happened in the intervening years. The point I want to make is that it's a totally different matter now to say withdraw, with all the implications of that withdrawal for a lot of other countries, and for the meaning of our other commitments."

"I understand that. But I'm interested in knowing what you think about the soundness of what was done then, years ago. As late as 1960 or 1961, the public had hardly even heard of Indo-China or Vietnam. And then Kennedy started talking about it, and then the *Times* started saying that we were losing the war. Before that, Vietnam could have disappeared from the face of the earth and the American public would hardly have noticed. What if we had *not* set up SEATO? What if we had just let France be defeated and pull out, and just let whatever powers were in play take their course?"

"Well, I think the process makes sense as a process," Rostow said. "As an integral part of an effort we were making in all parts of the world to recreate some kind of system of order. What we did to help the French in Indo-China, to help the British in Malaysia, can't be understood, I think, except as part of our general policy toward Britain and France and our efforts to create a Europe. From the beginning of the Marshall Plan, the United States saw very clearly that Europe was weak and fragmented, that a constructive future for Germany lay only in deep association with the other European states as part of a European union of some kind, and that only a European union confronting the enormous mass of the Soviet Union would have the strength and stability to flourish and to defend itself. The paradox of the nuclear weapon is that Europe is today more dependent on us than it was in 1949—that Europe can defend itself effectively only if the nuclear weapon somehow is put back into the bottle. But it remains true, I think, that our effort to encourage the creation of a European unity was a sound effort, conceived in terms of our own national interest to try to stabilize Europe as a counterweight to Russia."

"I can understand that part of the argument, but—"

"Now France went back into Indo-China. President Roosevelt was very dubious about it, but General De-Gaulle insisted on it."

"Roosevelt was against it, wasn't he?"

"Well, he was more or less against, but of course he died. But if France wanted to do this, then we had our relations with France to consider and the central importance of Europe to our own security. And we went through the period with Suez and Indo-China and Algeria with terrific blows to our relations with France, and we've suffered from those wounds, too. Nonetheless, what was done was done, I think, in very large part to try to help build Europe and to try to coöperate with France and Britain, and out of concern that these smaller states in Southeast Asia would go down like dominoes, in the famous expression, if the process of

32

expansion weren't halted somewhere. It reminds me a little bit of the great debate in the thirties about Danzig. The word went around Europe, 'Why should we die for Danzig?' But if the resistance to Hitler's expansion had come earlier it would have been easier to contain. The phenomenon of a balance of power doesn't depend so much on any particular piece of territory, I think, as on getting acceptance for the notion of equilibrium and for the notion that there can't be expansion through force, expansion by unilateral decision, because you can't tell where it's going to end."

I asked whether we had gone into Indo-China, then, because of our relationship with France or because we believed that Southeast Asia was important to an international balance of power.

"For both reasons, I think," Rostow said. "I think you can find both reflected in what was said and done at the time—a time, remember, when there were hostilities going on all over Asia. And then the Tonkin Gulf Resolution affirmed that the independence of Southeast Asia is important to the security of the United States. Well, what is the independence of Southeast Asia? You can say that no one country is important but that the whole collection of countries may be important, dominating the approaches to India, Indonesia—which is a big and important country—Australia, and New Zealand. So the conviction grew up that at a given point the process of Communist expansion had to be stopped.

33

Now, you see, Korea is somewhat different, because South Korea is close to Japan, and has always been an integral part of the defense of Japan. And you'll notice what President Nixon and Prime Minister Sato have said on the subject. They have reaffirmed the importance of the independence of South Korea to the security of Japan. Now, that's a tangible historical fact that can be recognized, although we found it just as disagreeable to go into Korea as we do to be in South Vietnam."

"Was that our main reason for going into Korea— her importance in relation to Japan?"

"I think that was part of it, but not the whole of it. I think it was the feeling of the President and of Congress that if we didn't stop this kind of deliberate attack— which was sponsored by the Soviet Union in that case— we would have to stop it elsewhere. And that, as in Europe, we would come to the point, after all the agreements we had made with the Russians had been broken and they were clearly in a process of expansion, at which we would simply have to draw the line somewhere and resist on it."

"All right, that one's easier to understand; armies were marching across a border. But back to France and Indo-China. What if we had said, 'No, this is not the same situation, and Southeast Asia doesn't make that much difference. Let the dominoes fall.' What might have happened? What are we afraid of?"

Rostow said, "I suppose we're afraid of a conviction's

spreading in that part of the world that there is no possibility of resistance, and afraid that the enormous masses and the geographical and strategic areas of that region will fall into the hands of hostile or potentially hostile powers."

"Do people in that region look at this as one process? Are all these countries just the same? Don't they have internal politics?"

"Oh, yes, of course they have. I'm convinced, after talking with a lot of people from those countries, that they *do* regard this process as a Communist effort— not coördinated, not centrally planned, necessarily, but assisted, and powerfully assisted, by China and by Hanoi."

"They regard it as an effort that, if it succeeded, would work to the benefit of China?" I asked.

"That's right."

"That would materially enlarge China's—"

"Range of influence. Now, I think the other—"

"Would it make her stronger militarily or economically? Or just more influential?"

"Well, some of those areas are reasonably rich in food production, as Vietnam is. Malaysia is rich in other ways."

"But would it give China something to use against us?"

"Yes," Rostow said. "And it would mean that a philosophy of resistance and independence was hopeless. Some of those countries in Southeast Asia are extremely weak, like Cambodia and Laos—and Burma, which has been suffering a good deal from incursions from the Chinese side. The big country, of course, is India. Now, there is a strategic element in this, if we can ever try to think separately about the naval problem and the nuclear problem. The base at Cam Ramh Bay and the whole strategic position of South Vietnam have always been regarded as critical to attempts to control Southeast Asia. The Japanese occupied the Bay region, you remember, before they went farther south, and the French kept it as a strategic point of great importance. And that, I think, is a legitimate part of our calculation. Similarly, the independence of Cambodia, Thailand, and Burma is important to the defense of India.

"But I think the major concern—at least, my major concern—in this miserable affair is the long-range impact a withdrawal would have on Japanese policy. Japanese policy is a matter of the utmost importance to the future of world politics. Japan is the third industrial nation of the world, and our policy toward Japan has been one of close coöperation, and I think it should remain one of close coöperation. Close and deep coöperation. I think the ultimate question, really, in that whole area, if we're going to try to preserve any kind of balance of power in Asia—which has always been a goal of American policy—is how China is going to be modernized. If we're going to pull away from Asia and let Asia stew in its own juice, then I think one of the things to think about is how this process of modernizing China is going to be organized. Is it going to be carried out in the long run by the whole group of Western nations? By Russia alone? By Japan alone? By everybody working coöperatively, as is now the case, pretty much, in India? That would be the best solution of all. That is a series of questions in which we have an *immense* national interest. And I think the outcome of the Vietnam war has a good deal to do with the calculations that Japan will make about the validity of American guarantees and about the conclusions that can be drawn from American guarantees."

"You're saying that we have this big interest in Japan because she's the one real power in Asia—the only industrial power."

"China is a nuclear power, though, and potentially a very great power in other ways," Rostow said.

"But Japan is a real modern power, an industrial, technological power. And she's a big trading partner of the West. Couldn't she exist as a capitalist, democratic country side by side with Communist countries in the area, the way Western Europe exists side by side with Eastern Europe?"

"I'm not talking ideologically—about whether a country is Communist or not. I'm talking about a power constellation, about the possibility of peace. Will Japan remain closely associated with us—deeply linked to us in the realm of politics, of the conduct of foreign relations—or will she go off on a course that's totally different, if we pull away?"

"Don't those political affiliations follow the economic ones?"

"No."

"They don't? Well, then economic affiliation with us is no guarantee that the political one would remain."

"None whatever. Any more than it was in the case of Germany."

"On the other hand, some economic affiliation with China wouldn't necessarily mean a political affiliation."

"Not a bit. Not at all. No, I'm talking about—"

"Then what are we afraid of from Japan? I realize that some people look at her as sort of the Germany of Asia, because of her history. But say she does develop a political and economic affiliation with China. What are the Japanese going to do to us? Are they going to invade us? Or is she so important to us economically?"

"I think the future relationship between Japan and China is one of the critical questions of the world," Rostow said. "Now, Japan is Japan. It's a powerful, well-governed society, and a very rational one. After the Japanese lost the war, they reached certain conclusions, the principal one being that it was infinitely better to coöperate with the United States than to follow a hostile, militaristic line. Now, it's greatly to our interest to have that judgment proved correct. And I think Vietnam is tied into that process. I don't mean that Vietnam is the only key to it. But I think that if we pull out of Vietnam and the place is taken over by Hanoi, and Hanoi then takes over Laos and Cambodia, and there's trouble in Burma and in the northern part of India and in Malaysia—then I think the Japanese will draw certain conclusions from that situation. And I think their policy will take on a much more nationalistic cast."

What are some specific kinds of things that could follow from that?"

"I think the first thing that would happen would be that they wouldn't ratify the nuclear-nonproliferation treaty. They would feel compelled to become a nuclear power."

"O.K. So then you've got one more nuclear power to worry about."

"That's right, and that is a lot in itself. And I think that this would mean a very different political posture and a temptation to the Japanese to reach some sort of understanding with China; and the Chinese, for their part, might find such a collaboration tempting as a counterweight to the Russians. This could mean combinations and coalitions that could result in a basically new pattern that would dominate the whole evolution of Asia."

"Let's say that that happens," I said. "China is successful, she feeds her population, she builds up her industry, she goes ahead with her nuclear program, and she becomes allied with Japan. China and Japan have taken over all of Asia. What can they do to us as a result of that? I don't see how that manpower and land make any difference today as far as war goes. I keep wondering if these analogies with Europe and with the past make any sense. At one time, it made sense, of a kind, for Germany or Japan to start a war. It was something manageable. It was just people shooting each other and dropping some bombs. It didn't mean blowing up the world. Power is different now, with nuclear weapons. No one wants to start a nuclear war. So what could they do to us?"

"You keep supposing that the existence of nuclear weapons is magic, and that we can stay home in safety, threatening invaders with them," Rostow said. "I don't think that's true at all. I think the existence of nuclear weapons complicates problems, but doesn't remove them. Unless the Russians and the Chinese change their policy entirely, peace can be achieved only through equilibrium at the level of conventional diplomacy and conventional force. So we come back to the first question you asked, which I think is the right question. What is our foreign policy about? Are we interested only in protecting ourselves against the risk of being invaded, or, as the world gets smaller and smaller, do we have an interest in trying to preserve what Senator Fulbright called a world of wide horizons, a world in which we can move around and trade and travel on a large scale, and, basically, live as we're living now? If the change you are talking about should occur, that fact could impose on us, in the first place, an enormous military cost. If you look at the consequences of the Soviet Revolution in Russia or the Communist takeover of China, you'll see that the cost to us has been prodigious—in maintaining a military establishment, maintaining forces abroad, maintaining bases to try to contain that expansionist pressure—and that cost would be doubled and redoubled.

"Why would it?"

"Because the arithmetic of power would change."

"We've reached a standoff with Russia in Europe, but what we were trying to do there was keep Russia from expanding into Western Europe. Now, in this model I just asked you to consider, we've *given* the rest of Asia, so to speak, to Japan and China. What are we trying to keep them from expanding into, then? They've got Asia, and then there are the United States and Western Europe, and Russia and Eastern Europe. There's almost no place for anyone to go."

"Well, if the world remained in that condition, that would be fine."

"You would have some sort of balance, of which I don't understand the disadvantages, unless they're economic ones that I know nothing about," I said. "I can see that there would have been great economic problems for us if Western Europe had gone. They're our natural trading partners. I know that Japan is a big partner, but there's no similar stake over there economically, is there?"

"The economics of it are real, but not central, I think. The older I get, the less of an economic determinist I become. There was no economic reason for Hitler to have gone on his rampage of conquest. He could have

41

made infinitely more money by trading than by trying to conquer."

Rostow lit a cigarette and sat in silence for a minute or so. Then he said, "The problem is the fear of military threat that a great slide in the distribution of military power always precipitates. My thinking comes back to the kind of situation that precipitates war. The danger of war becomes acute when people fear they're losing the possibility of controlling their own fate. The Cold War began in Iran right after the Second World War—when the Russians moved into the northern provinces of Iran. We reacted very sharply. That is exactly the kind of expansion we can see at work now in the Middle East, and it's extremely dangerous, because it has in it the seeds of an explosion that could involve us with the Russians. Here you have a process extending over very large parts of the world which could suddenly be denied to us. When a war between Greece and Turkey was threatened back in '67, and the Turks were ready to go, they restricted access to their air space. There was no way for American planes to get from Asia to Europe. There were planes stacked up in Tehran, and we didn't have any alternate route. We were totally dependent on Turkey. And this was a disturbing situation. If too many strategic areas of the world come under hostile control, that begins to engender the kinds of political fears, the kinds of anxieties, that move men to war. You can say this is irrational. If we just looked at the situation and kept our cool, we wouldn't have to react. That course might be correct sometimes. But there are real risks in such a process nonetheless. The question arises as to when people find the risks intolerable, as we did in the Cuban missile crisis. Now, the Cuban missile crisis wasn't created by the government. It exploded, and the government handled it in a certain way. The information, as you said, became generally available, and it created a wave of panic."

"I know. But what if something similar came up now, something that did not threaten us technologically, and the President and the State Department just remained calm and explained to the country that nothing had really changed? It seems to me that you explain the system in terms of the system. You say we do it this way because that's the way it's done."

"The trouble is really a deeper one," Rostow said. "We know that Soviet policy and Chinese policy are not as benign as all that. We know that they do probe and reach very far—throughout the Middle East, throughout Africa, throughout Asia, of course, and into South America. And in this country there is a fear— which no one can say is irrational—that the aim of their policies is not simply to consolidate power within three great blocks, as you suggest, but to reach all the way."

"They want to control the world?"

"As much of it as they can. If you're responsible for the safety of the United States, you say, 'Well, the risk is that we have to fight a lot of little campaigns to try to stabilize the world more or less as we can see it evolving, with India getting stronger, Korea getting stronger, Japan getting stronger and more stable.' We can imagine living in that world as a free, progressive society at home. But if we say that we're going to risk allowing these enormous masses of people, resources, strategic locations to be taken over by governments that openly proclaim their hostility to us as a matter of ideology, and their desire to reduce or control our freedom—that we're going to allow a situation of power to evolve in the world in which Europe would be neutral, the way Finland is neutral, and in which Japan would become part of a hostile bloc—then you're dealing with fears that you can't say are irrational.

"That's the whole trouble. I think your questions are absolutely right. This is the guts of the problem. Why do we care about a balance of power? It's a tradition in foreign policy. Maybe everybody is mouthing the same old formula out of habit. But we care about it because of the fear that in the international system dominant power will be exercised by someone who is hostile. The statesmen of the past have always said they were concerned not with intentions but with capacities. And that's what you're really talking about—the evolution of capacities in hostile hands. And there's plenty of evidence of hostility all over the world to give fuel to those fears. Now, you can say, 'Oh, they'll calm down,' or 'They'll realize it's much more sensible to trade with us than to fight us,' but how can anybody be sure that this will happen? Isn't it much better to try to prevent a constellation of power from evolving that could support such a program? After all, if your guesses were wrong, the consequences of inaction would be irreversible, except at the cost of an unthinkable war."

"I can understand that, but I think we got off the track of what I was trying to ask. I wasn't willing to give Russia anything she wanted, to let Europe become another Finland. I was having us preserve our interest in—"

"The Middle East."

"Well, the Middle East. I don't understand that, either. There's oil. But let's leave out the Middle East for the moment. We're going to go ahead and preserve our interest in Europe and in Latin America, and we've conceded Eastern Europe to Russia, and now I'm conceding Asia to China and Japan. I'm trying to get past the vagueness of 'power constellation' and 'hostility,' and get you to give me some concrete examples of what might happen if this change came about. Aside from the traditional response that it just doesn't seem like a good idea. Aside from the fears that would be aroused in our public as one country after another fell to the Communists. In terms of real power, economic or military, how would we be affected?"

"There would be two things about such a situation that would cause terrific alarm, as similar movements have in the past," Rostow replied. "The first thing would be the question: Where will the process of expansion end? And then: Can it be stopped if it gets going with great momentum? You know perfectly well that if Australia were threatened, we would react. We wouldn't stand by and see the Australians slaughtered."

"But would Australia be threatened? Is there something in Australia that China and Japan might want?"

"Why did Japan bomb Australia in the Second World War?"

"I don't know."

"I don't think you can get at this phenomenon by finding an economic rationale. We're spending an incredible amount of money on the defense of South Vietnam, for which there can be no economic justification whatever. We don't profit economically from the balance of power. What we get from it is a sense of security."

"But China must feel insecure surrounded by nuclear arms and bases. Maybe the Chinese have the same fears we have."

"Well, you know, nobody noticed that our policy toward China in the United Nations changed in 1966," Rostow said. "I was instrumental in proposing that we change our posture on the U.N. vote about China. And the President agreed, and we did it. We thought there would be a hell of an outcry in the country, but it was taken as normal. Nobody noticed it. We voted for three years in a row in support of a resolution to study the China question. Now, the reason we came up with that—we thought at first we were going to come up with a much bolder resolution about seating China—was because of the complications of the Security Council and the Formosa question. So we said we'd support a study resolution which would put this thing in motion. The minute we made that position clear in New York, a lot of countries that had been lying very low on this question—particularly Japan—became very active in defeating the study motion. We voted with the Belgians and the Italians and a number of other countries. And the Russians, of course, were simply bewildered by this change, or frightened of it, because they saw it as a sign that we were trying to cosy up to China at their expense. But it was defeated nonetheless.

"Now, we've gone to terrific lengths to reassure the Chinese about their own security. I'm in favor of doing more, if they are willing. We've probably had more diplomatic contact with the Chinese than anybody else has, through these meetings at Warsaw. They understand the restraint with which we conducted the campaigns in Korea and Vietnam. They understand the change in our position on China at the U.N., and other signals of our purpose. It's very hard for me to imagine that at the level of rationality they anticipate military hostility from us."

"But they must feel the same way. They must find it hard to imagine that we would anticipate military hostility from them."

"No, not with a growing nuclear power. Their policy —verbally, at least—is very active. You find the Chi-

47

nese trying to foment revolution all over Africa, the Middle East, and Southeast Asia."

"But they haven't really done anything. They talk a lot. When is the last time they lost a man—besides those border skirmishes with Russia?"

"Korea, I suppose."

"When I said maybe we ought to make *them* feel more secure, I didn't mean by chatting with them in Warsaw. Because we don't feel more secure from that, either. We feel secure with alliances, and with space between us and other people."

"I agree with you. But isn't that precisely what our restraint about North Vietnam means?"

"We wouldn't feel secure if we were surrounded by bases, the way they are."

"Well, we have Castro, of course," Rostow said, smiling.

"But presumably the Russian missiles are gone from Cuba."

"Presumably. Or they have become much less important."

"Maybe China and Japan would see their expansion in Asia just as we see our influence in Latin America and Western Europe," I said. "But you believe that if we did allow nature to take its course, and one of them did take over all of Asia, she might do something—"

"Very rash."

"She might be willing to have a nuclear war and start the world all over again?"

"That's right."

48

"Is that what people in the government have been afraid of in the past?" I asked. "Is that what Rusk and Johnson worried about?"

"Well, I can tell you what Rusk and *I* were worried about," Rostow said. "We used to sit and have a drink two or three times a week at the end of the day and ruminate about problems of this kind and try to find alternative paths."

"But did he question the premises that I'm asking about?"

"Oh, very much. Rusk is very curious that way. He kept reading. When he'd go to bed at night, he'd read for a half or three-quarters of an hour—a new book or article in the field—and he'd often call my attention to a book I hadn't seen. No, he was trying desperately to find alternative paths out of this dilemma. And he asked me as a new boy in the system to try to think unthinkable thoughts. I suppose the answer is that in terms of responsibility or partial responsibility for the conduct of American foreign relations you say, on one side, that there's a hell of a risk in this Vietnam war and the alienation of the American people from it, and the implication that this might feed the fires of isolationism. Well, why are we afraid of isolationism? Because of a fear that if we pulled back, and the world started to slip around toward neutralism and new combinations of power, the situation might become very threatening in atmosphere, and some episode here, there, or elsewhere could precipitate a general war.

"For instance, take North Korea. The North Koreans

49

are absolutely *wild* characters. And they've been restrained only by the most *dire* threats. I should be willing to bet that in the event of a pullout in South Vietnam
one of the first things you'd see would be a big blowup
in Korea. What do we do about that? We're angry at
the Koreans anyway, because of the Pueblo episode.
There was a lot of rage in the country about that. And
my guess is that if the Koreans acted up the Americans
would hit very hard. *Very* hard. That would be natural,
and human, but it might be dangerous. What are the
Russians going to do? To say nothing of the Chinese.
Korea is right at the front door of Japan—a much more
dangerous place in many ways than Vietnam. President
Johnson was always much more concerned, in a way,
about the Middle East than about Vietnam, because he
said it involved the risk of a confrontation with Russia,
not with China. In the Middle East you have a situation that's damn near anarchy, and almost impossible
to control. The Russians talked with us calmly and
rationally about trying to reach an agreement with
Israel and all that, but they kept on sending missiles
and planes and one thing or another."

"We don't know what strangeness lurks in the Chinese, but we feel pretty sure the Russians don't want
nuclear war with us, don't we?" I asked.

"Yes, but confrontation is a very tricky thing," Rostow
said. "They won't confront us, but we don't confront
them, either. When the Middle Eastern war ap-
proached Syria, that's when the hot line went into

effect. The Russians said it was becoming a class war. Now, we put *terrific* pressure on the Israelis to stop. I can't tell you how many Middle Eastern diplomats who'd been taking a devoutly Arab line in the U.N. and elsewhere came to me in the summer of '67 and, in my office or at lunch, said, 'Well, the Israelis have failed.' And I'd ask what they meant, and they'd say, 'We were hoping they would occupy Damascus and Cairo.' They can't occupy Damascus or Cairo today, because the Russians are there.

"When I came into the State Department, in 1966, Rusk asked me to try to think of alternatives in Vietnam, and I thought of the way the Korean war was unwound. And I told the Russians, with full backing from my bosses, that this was the best way to solve the Vietnam problem—the way the Korean problem was solved. Namely, by Russian-American collaboration. They said, 'That's very interesting, and it hasn't been rejected, but it's very difficult for us.' And I said, 'Yes, we understand, we're not trying to push you out of there and turn it over to the Chinese at all. Quite the contrary.' And they said, 'We never reject this approach.' But they didn't act on it, either. Although now they're claiming some credit for having pushed Hanoi to the bargaining table.

"They are very much concerned about leadership of the world Communist movement, or movements, and their rivalry with China in that regard. They really seem to care quite a lot about that. What are the implications of that for us? You're not dealing only with Rus-

51

sia; you're dealing with Russia plus something—a Communist ideological component that is hard to predict. George Kennan once said that it was a mistake to think that the serious men who direct the Communist movement of the world can be diverted by politeness or the way in which they're treated. You must have respect for them. They really mean it. I don't know how much they mean it, but they seem to mean it quite a lot. I don't think the Russian position in Vietnam makes any sense from the national point of view. From the national point of view, they ought to be doing in Vietnam what they're doing in India. That is to say, pursuing a policy parallel to our own policy and hostile to China. That's what they're doing now with the Indians. We welcome that. Soviet military aid, technical missions, factories—fine. That's great, because there, clearly, our interests and their interests are the same— for the moment, anyway: to try to keep the Chinese from taking over India. Maybe the Chinese would get so embroiled in India that they would never pick themselves up, but that's not a risk you can take."

"Speaking of India, if we're willing to spend so much to try to create a democracy in Vietnam, why don't we do more to help India, which is the largest democracy in the world?"

"I don't, of course, agree with the implication of your question," Rostow said. "I should argue that our interest is not to protect democracy as such but to deter, prevent, or defeat aggression. But our interest in India is profound, as we indicated some years ago, when a Chinese attack on India was threatened, and by our actions in the India-Pakistan dispute. India, of course, has chosen a non-aligned position in world politics. But our aid programs in India are enormous. I've forgotten the statistics, but they are surely among the largest and best conceived in our whole aid effort. And we mobilized the international assistance which saved India from famine in 1966 and 1967, and have worked effectively to help India's agriculture, birth-control program, and industrialization."

THREE

Africa and the Middle East

"What about the opinions of someone like George Kennan, who is a conservative and a balance-of-power man, and who had so much to do with the whole idea of containment?" I asked.

"Which he now denies."

"That's not the impression I got from reading his *Memoirs*. He just doesn't like the form the policy took. He thought there was a threat from Russia, but he didn't think it was as military as everyone else did. He says the application of the containment idea was too sweeping—that it shouldn't be applied everywhere in the world. He says that there are only five areas of the world—the United States, the United Kingdom, The Rhine Valley, the Soviet Union, and Japan—where modern military strenth can be produced, that only one of them is under Communist Control, and that our job is to see to it that none of the others come under Communist control."

"I've always had the greatest difficulty in trying to parse George's articles and books," Rostow replied. "He said, for example, that the long-term risk of Soviet penetration in the Middle East was not great, because Muslims would never accept Communist protection. It comes down to this—many people say we're safe as long as we keep these enormous industrial islands in the world within our control. That is to say, if we and Western Europe and Japan remain linked, then the rest of the world can go to hell, because we'll have enough power. To which President Johnson's answer always was 'These fellows forget that eighty per cent of the people in the world are colored, and that we simply can't expect to live safely in a big white house on a hill, with everyone underneath starving and milling around, or in tyranny, or under hostile control.' It just isn't going to work that way."

"I see assertions like that in the press all the time, offered with no explanation and implying 'You know what *this* could lead to.' But I don't. I could understand that warning if we were the only rich family in some town and everyone was going to come storming up, but how does this work in terms of nations? Leaving aside humanitarian concerns for the moment, what are those poor people going to *do* to us—those poor nations, which are getting weaker?"

"We can't really leave humanitarian considerations out of the equation. Our problem is not only peace but the kind of world we want to live in. Johnson cared

56

passionately about world poverty and hunger, not for
security reasons but because he is an idealist, and believed we should help because we are rich and they are
poor. I feel the same way. But there is a security
dimension to the problem. I agree that your hard question should be answered in its own terms. The Chinese
are *not* getting weaker. At least, they're getting nuclear
power. President Johnson once said, 'Some of these
people tell me that Asians are not our kind of people.'
That's Bill Fulbright: 'Lyndon, they're not our kind of
people. Why are we worrying about these Asiatics?'
And I think the worst thing I can possibly imagine for
the future of the world is a combination of the white
powers, including Russia, against the people of color.
Then you'd have ideological considerations mixed up
with problems of race, and you'd have a mess that
would be almost untouchable, I should think."

"I see what you're talking about, but—"

"You can say that these are only reasons of prudence—
maybe irrational fear of the unknown, if you will.
They're not. They are reasons of decency and humanity
as well. But the unknown is a real aspect of the problem. If you stop our attempt to build a system of peace
in the world, this is the kind of concern that you begin
to face. George Kennan criticized the Truman Doctrine
on that ground that it was too universal. Well, it was
universal in form, but it hasn't been universal in fact.
We haven't intervened in Eastern Europe. We didn't
intervene in Czechoslovakia, or, before that, in Hungary

57

or East Germany. God knows, freedom was at stake there. But that wasn't the point. Neither have we intervened in dozens of wars, coups d'état and takeovers where the extension of Soviet power or Chinese power was not an issue. Mr. Rusk used to keep score on his desk; he used to compile statistics on the number of coups d'état he had lived through. There were about two a month. They were constantly taking place, all over the world, and some of them involved a lot of fighting."

"Your former colleague George Ball asks in *The Discipline of Power* if that kind of scorekeeping really means anything—if all these changes *are* an extension of Russian or Chinese power, or if they might not in fact be liabilities. What have you got when you've got a country that's falling apart, that may not even be a real country?"

"You may not have anything at all in one case, and you may have a lot if the countries are all combined," Rostow said. "The Russians are deeply entrenched in Syria, Egypt, Algeria, the Sudan. Now, you can say, 'It's expensive for them, just as Castro is expensive for them, and let's let them stew in their own juice. Let them discover that empire doesn't pay.' Norman Angell pointed that out in 1910, in *The Great Illusion*. His book was a best-seller, and he was eventually knighted and awarded the Nobel Peace Prize. Everybody read the book, and nobody believed it. From the economic point of view, he was absolutely right. Empire *never*

58

pays. Jeremy Bentham pointed this out in the eighteenth century. So, you'd argue, if the Russians want to go on an imperialist binge, let them. And they'll discover it's very expensive, and the Russians *hate* to spend money. Fine. If Russian imperialism were all that was involved, I'd say great. But the implications of Soviet policy in the Middle East raise tremendous security problems for the defense of Europe, and they also raise the possibility of an explosion that would touch the nerves of humanity—I mean, if Israel were wiped out . . . It's nothing you can play with."

"But, to get back to Johnson's white house on the hill, and leaving the Middle East out of it for the moment, what if all the colored nations *were* aligned? It seems incredible that they ever would be. But what if they were aligned with China? What could they do to us?"

"Aligned with China plus Japan."

"O.K., China plus Japan. I grant you that Japan would give such a bloc more power, but would all these other nations that Johnson is worried about because they're colored? What are they going to *do* to us? Would they float all those people over here on rafts, or what?" Rostow laughed, and I said, "I don't mean to be facetious. I just don't understand. Is it more fear of the unknown, or has somebody in some room at the Pentagon figured out what might happen to us? Does Herman Kahn have a theory about what all those colored people could do?"

59

"You mean vast cannon fodder transported in ships and landing on the coast of California?"

"Or whatever. Is anybody thinking about that?"

"If anyone is, I've never seen his lucubrations," Rostow said. "The risk, I should say, is that the process you describe could get to the point at which it would precipitate a general counterreaction, which takes place almost by instinct, and which can increase the risk of war."

"That's that irrational thing."

"Yes, if you want to describe it that way. But you're dealing with a phenomenon—war and peace—which is not wholly rational. That's the trouble."

"This is a very depressing conversation," I said. "The way you describe the workings of foreign affairs is much more frightening than any of the theories that I hear from the left. The left always assumes that this country has some kind of—"

"Deep economic interest, yes. We're out to make a fortune out of South Vietnam, and we're willing to spend thirty billion a year. Boy, that's some fortune!"

"Well, to continue with this business of the colored nations," I said. "Why don't we let the Russians have Africa, if you're worried about a colored alliance against us? That would save us some money, and it would be a counter to China."

"I'm not worried about a colored alliance against us, a new Yellow or Black Peril, because I don't believe that America can or should wash its hands of the problem of helping the new nations in their development," Rostow said. "But, in the terms of your narrow question, I suppose you're right."

"Well, it's the narrow concern that I'm trying to get at—the power relationships. In that way, what would be wrong with letting the Russians 'have' Africa?"

"We've been very passive about Africa. I don't think we've been doing enough there, myself. But, again, tensions can build up, and build up pretty acutely. Take the Nigerian affair. At first, our attitude was 'Let the British take care of it, it's not our concern.' Then it went to hell. And then it became insoluble. We tried to help resolve it through diplomacy, through the Emperor of Ethiopia and the Organization of African Unity. The Africans didn't want it to come to the U.N. They wanted to deal with it themselves."

"What's the British and Russian interest there, in Nigeria?"

"The British are interested in Nigeria because she's part of the British Commonwealth. They're hooked."

"I mean some other reason."

"Well, you know, that's an important reason. That's why people function."

"What about the Russians, then?"

"Russia moved into Nigeria through Egypt and otherwise, as another way of expanding her influence and control in a pretty sensitive area of Africa."

"But to what end?"

"The smaller states around Nigeria are alarmed about

61

the Russian and Egyptian penetration of Nigeria. And these states came to us with hair-raising tales. They said we should do something about Nigeria and Biafra, and then it became impossible to do anything, because the African states were totally divided. It was the God-damnedest mess you ever saw."

"But why does Russia care about it? Is she just seeking influence?"

"That's right. The Russians want to spread the gospel as far as they can spread it, as I see it. They have a great interest in the Persian Gulf, which I expect will be the focus of one of the most difficult crises of the next five years. The British are pulling out of the Persian Gulf."

"You don't think the Russians have some—"

"Master plan?"

"Well, just something specific they want."

"No. No."

"Economic interest, or—"

"No. It's control they're after. Of course, the Persian Gulf is very tempting, because the oil in the Middle East is still vital to Europe and to Japan. We've liberated ourselves from the sheikhs, and maybe the discoveries in Alaska will liberate everybody else. But the oil in the Middle East is vital to Europe, and perhaps the most important event that has occurred in recent months in that connection is the takeover in Libya. There was a coup in Libya by officers who seem to be close to Egypt. Now, if Nasser should control Libya, he'd really be home free. Because that country is just a pool of money! The most unbe*lievable* place that ever was! The society is weak, and small. Many of the school-teachers there are Egyptian anyway. And the country has more oil than you can imagine."

"Well, that's something rational. You can understand something like that."

"But that frightens the bejesus out of Tunisia. Tunisia could be caught between Algeria and Libya. If Libya became a hostile power, Tunisia would feel threatened. Now, if the whole North African coast is in the hands of Nasser, acting for the Russians, and if there are Russian air and naval bases there, then France and Italy begin to get very much alarmed. You could have a situation in which the Russians could say to us any morning, 'Liquidate NATO and get out of Europe.' You see, that's the risk you're looking at."

"Why could they say that to us?"

"Because they would be in a position to threaten all kinds of things. In the first place, they could cut off the oil. Right after the Middle East war in 1967, when there was an Arab boycott of oil shipments, Europe came within five minutes of imposing rationing. It was that serious. Luckily, the Iranians continued to sell oil to Europe, the boycott collapsed, and that was enough."

"Well, apart from the emotional issue of Israel," I said, "the whole thing in the Middle East as far as the West is concerned is oil—is that right?"

"And strategic space. Nearness to Europe."

"It sounds like—"

"It sounds like an insane world," Rostow said. "And it is."

"I was going to say that, from much of what you've said, it sounds as if the balance-of-power theory were based not on a fear of results that we can imagine but on a fear of something that we *can't* imagine. We don't have a specific fear—it's just fear of the unknown."

"It isn't all unknown. The real question is whether Russian policy or Chinese policy is going to be rational and coöperative or whether it's going to be expansionist and hostile and revolutionary. And the second thing about the problem is that many of these countries are controlled by people who are willing to take wild risks. Nasser and the fellows in Korea and Hanoi—their world is centered on themselves. And they're in a position to force policies on the Russians which we often think the Russians don't really want. I'm not sure that's true, but that's the impression we get. Then the Russians get into a position where they have to defend their satellite. Now, in a way that's the scariest part of the problem."

"Why do the great powers put themselves in that position, when it doesn't involve some really vital strategic or economic interest?"

"Well, *why?* That's a real question. What are the Russians doing in the Middle East? Why are the Russians giving Nasser all this stuff? *They* know Nasser. I've often said it was like giving a—"

"You just told me why—money, and strategic consequences for Europe," I said.

"Yes."

✦✦✦✦✦✦✦✦✦✦✦✦✦✦✦✦✦✦✦✦✦✦✦✦✦✦✦✦✦✦✦✦✦✦✦✦✦

FOUR

The Irrational Factor

As I did so often during our talks, I returned now to my question about the irrational factor in war, and to my effort to get from Rostow a concrete example of what we feared from a shift in the balance of power in Asia. "If I understand you," I said, "when our government leaders think about the possibility that all of Asia might come under hostile control, they haven't worked out some model for what might happen to us. It's just that it doesn't sound like a good idea for—"

"It's a traditional attitude toward—"

"You just can't tell what might happen. But our government doesn't have any theories about it. Is that right?"

"No, there is a theory about the risks of hegemonic power. That idea has always been the animating force of our foreign policy, of British foreign policy, and of everybody else's foreign policy. It's a terrible comment on the nature of the world political system. Sometimes students say, 'We want to study things that are *relevant* to our problems.' I say, more than half seriously, that they ought to study the organization of the Roman Empire. That was the last time we had a general system of peace in the world."

"The European part of your explanation is easy to understand, because—"

"But in 1941 we suffered a very severe blow from a Japanese power that was interested in conquest, in driving us out of the Pacific. Our Pacific instincts have always been as strong as our European instincts."

"But why do we have the same interest in the Pacific that we have in Europe?"

"The same kinds of fears."

"But in Europe it's not just fear. We *know* some of the things that could have happened if Western Europe had gone to the Russians, don't we?"

"Do we know? Do we know what would have happened if Hitler had conquered Europe or if—"

"No, I don't mean we know what *would* have happened, but we can think of some things that *could* have happened and that we didn't want to happen."

"That's my point. It applies just as much to the East as to the West. Our fear isn't economic. We could probably continue to trade with Europe, as we do with Finland. But then we'd have the whole defense burden ourselves—we wouldn't have any strong allies. The idea that all of Europe's resources and manpower, skill and technology could come within the ambit of Soviet control causes concern. Now, you can say that's an irrational concern, and you may be right. I don't happen to think so. But if it is, it's the kind of irrational concern that has moved governments as long as there have been governments."

"But you can work out some hypothetical situations and deduce some rational fears from that—"

"The calculus of population and skill and education, yes."

"Right. But it's hard to work out the same rational hypothesis for Asia that—"

"No, it isn't, not at all," Rostow said. "Japan is an enormous industrial country moving ahead very rapidly, and China— After all, the people of China are just as intelligent and able as the people of Japan. And there are a lot more of them."

"If Russia had taken over Europe, would your fears have been primarily military?"

"Yes, they would have been. In the sense that you would face threats that you couldn't accept. Such as 'We think it would be better if you had a Henry Wallace-type government.' You know—a *real* threat to your independence."

"But *how*, though? How could they make a threat like that? We'd tell them to go to hell. I always thought economics would be a large consideration."

"No, I think it's a different kind of perception. This, of course, is nothing that was much discussed during

73

my time in Washington, because this was taken as a premise, and everybody takes it as a premise—all the critics of our policy, and so on. Europe is the same civilization. You know, some frightful shock would occur to us if these people were brought under Russian control. But I think it's the calculus of power more than anything else. It's the fear of an overwhelming concentration of resources and skills and military potential brought under the control of a potentially hostile force."

"But when you make the analogy between Europe and Asia, there is a great economic difference, isn't there?"

"There is," Rostow said. "Except that things aren't static. We've seen what has happened to Japan in the last fifty years. And the same, or more, could happen to China. After all, the Chinese have developed a nuclear weapon—which takes a lot of industrial and scientific sophistication—awfully fast. They've run into some economic difficulties and setbacks in their program. But a very few years ago everybody was comparing China unfavorably to India, and now it's the other way around, as far as economic development is concerned. The military potential is there. And I think it's as old an instinct as there is in foreign policy, this anxiety and concern about hegemony."

"When you think about Europe in the thirties and forties, and armies marching across borders, and all that, you can imagine our being bombed or invaded, can't you?" I asked.

74

"Or threatened otherwise. Yes."

"But now, with the possibility of nuclear war, I don't see how Japan and China together, with Russia thrown in, could threaten us in any ultimate military way. In the way that, say, Hitler could have with a conquered Europe behind him, before weapons changed so much. I mean, are they going to give us some sort of ultimatum? We'd say, 'The hell with you! We're going to destroy your civilization.' "

"But the nuclear weapons can't be used, especially in that situation. That's precisely why I say I can't accept protection against *invasion* as the ultimate goal of our foreign policy. I think that if we faced that situation we would have to become a garrison state on a scale we can't even imagine now, and be concerned about threats from every quarter of the compass—be hemmed in. We couldn't be the kind of society we want to be."

"If what?"

"If we pulled back to the United States and concerned ourselves only with the risk of invasion, and the possibility of nuclear reprisal."

"But would there *be* any risk of invasion?"

"If you look at the development of naval power and the potentials for naval power that exist in Russia and Japan, and elsewhere, of course there would be a theoretical risk of invasion."

"But how? Would they be willing to take the risk of

threatening invasion when we have the ability to destroy them?"

"Well, the question is really how credible our nuclear weapons are."

"I think that if our back were against the wall, they'd be very credible," I said. "The Russians know that we won't use them for some small cause. But they know that if they sent battleships over here we would use the weapons. So what would be the military threat?"

"Are you sure we'd really bomb them if we were to be bombed in return? I'm not. I think the military threat would be that of trying to protect the United States in a world in which the balance of power was totally on the other side; in which there were no restraining forces on hegemonic powers, either in Asia or in Europe; in which we would live in a garrison. I think that's the fear."

"Not quite. I wasn't willing to give them Western Europe, in this hypothetical situation."

"But that threat has materialized now, in the course of events in the Middle East," Rostow said. "The neutralization of Europe is a real possibility. And so is the reduction of Western Europe to the political status of Finland. Anyway, by conceding my argument about Europe you really concede it all."

"You're being very patient with me, and I hate to keep coming back to the same point," I said. "But I don't agree that I've conceded the argument. This is all so vague. I'm trying to get something concrete, to

But if it's put to you in a totally different form, as it was to China— The tensions built up between China and Russia, and Russia very cleverly let it be known through questions raised in Eastern Europe, which they knew would get back to China, 'Well, we don't exclude a nuclear strike.' And they had a meeting. Now, you always have a meeting. But what's the subject matter of the meeting, and what are the terms of the understanding, and so forth? Disarmament? Coöperation? Can't you imagine people here urging the government to reach a reasonable compromise? I can."

"As you say, these problems are in some ways more psychological than they are economic, or even military."

"Absolutely. They're fundamentally psychological. What is security? How do you feel secure, in this kind of world, with this kind of hostility? The changes in the map of the world since 1945 have imposed a great strain on our minds. Americans are now struggling— struggling desperately—to digest the meaning of these enormous changes in the map of the world for their own lives. That's what the turbulence in our universities is really about, I think. That turbulence, and the deep agitation elsewhere in the country, reflects, I believe, the pain and difficulty of this battle between past and present in our minds. It is a demanding process. Can't we free ourselves of the fear of hegemony, the fear of being dominated, which has led men to war so often in the past? What does the fear of dominance do to people? Perhaps psychiatrists can answer

79

that question. I can't. All I know is that that kind of fear is a reality in human affairs. I don't think we are a new breed of men, immune to the diseases and fears of history. And I remain of the view that foreign policy should not allow such fears to develop, that the best —the only—cure for such fears is to prevent the convulsions in the distribution of power which have always been their cause. That's why I say that the nuclear bomb doesn't change the problem much, and that we have to continue to struggle patiently and steadily to get the Soviets and the Chinese to accept the notion of equilibrium which we have been seeking since 1947. Only on that basis can we hope for the kind of open, progressive world in which we could flourish as a free people—a world where energy could be devoted to development, and education, and social advance, and not to the tragedy and brutality of war. Everything turns on the outcome of the American debate about these themes."

"It seems that the best thing we could do for our security would be to help our potential enemies feel secure," I suggested.

"Of course. I agree completely. But how do you do it? One of the hardest things for people to realize— to believe—is that there are people in the world who don't *want* an agreement," Rostow said. "Our politics are politics of compromise, of accommodation, and it's very difficult for us to imagine that the Egyptians or the North Koreans or Hanoi or the Russians don't *want* to make an agreement. I was talking to some students the other day, and one of them said very earnestly, 'Well, why don't people try to reach an understanding with the Russians?' I answered, 'What on earth do you think we've been trying to do?' And I told him about some of our efforts in this direction—troop reductions in Europe, compromise in the Middle East, a solution in Vietnam, and so on. And he said, 'If I believe what you say, then I don't know what I believe about the world.' "

"We'd like to think that people had rational goals, even if they were evil."

"The world is absolutely nuts," Rostow said.

FIVE

"Is Chinese Policy Chinese?"

"Let me try a different approach," I said. "We've been talking about how threatening the world seems from our standpoint. Let's talk about how it must look to China."

"Yes, one of the things you should try to do is see a crisis from the other fellow's point of view," Rostow said. "That was one of the interesting aspects of President Johnson's method of policymaking. He would always designate somebody to be the devil's advocate, to come to some meeting prepared to represent the point of view of another country."

"Given the definition of security you've offered, it seems to me that if we were in China's position—with five hundred thousand foreign troops in Latin America, missile bases all around us, and no buffer states between us and hostile states—we would regard the situation as unacceptable. If you were a Chinese diplomat and

83

thought the way you think now, I believe you'd say that your country couldn't put up with what's going on now in Southeast Asia, whatever the history of it might be."

"Well, you forget that we've offered over and over again to withdraw entirely from South Vietnam, if the situation were suitably pacified. Just as we did from South Korea. Everybody forgets that we withdrew our forces from South Korea."

"But we're still there."

"We came *back* as a result of the war. I should think from the point of view of rational calculation, in terms of the Chinese attitude toward the Soviets, that if it were purely a Metternich game the Chinese would welcome a strong American presence in East Asia in the long run, as a guarantee against Soviety expansion in the north."

"On the other hand," I said, "she might see a danger of our combining with the Soviets and—"

"She *does*. She does very much. That's the accusation she makes, and I'm sure that has a psychological meaning for her. This interplay between three great Asian powers and a fourth, Japan, is the essence of the problem for the future—to manage that set of relations without consolidating a very hostile and overwhelming hegemony. And I think that's what we keep trying to do."

"But if you were a Chinese diplomat, would the situation in Asia look reasonable to you? Not just the presence of our troops but what we intend—that China remain within her borders while we're free to roam the world and have soldiers and bases everywhere."

"Well, I think you then have to face the question of whether the Chinese diplomat you're asking me to become for a moment is a nationalist or a revolutionary. Is Chinese policy Chinese? After all, China took over Tibet, and we did nothing. They had an ancient claim to Tibet. You asked about takeovers that don't result in any reaction—there was a major move on the Chinese part, which put them on the frontiers of India and put them in a different position in relation to Pakistan as well. And yet we did nothing and weren't terribly concerned. But first you have to tell me whether Chinese policy is dominated by considerations of national safety or revolutionary ambition. And this is a very puzzling and fascinating question."

"Well, of course, I don't know what their motivations are. But maybe they don't know whether we're motivated by considerations of national safety or we're capitalist revolutionaries, intent on spreading our notion of capitalism and liberal democracy everywhere."

"That's true," Rostow said. "They may or may not perceive that. There's not much excuse in terms of rationality for really believing that we're capitalist revolutionaries, and I can't believe that the responsible people in China believe that. For this reason: After the war, we demobilized, rather than trying to carry on a crusade. At the peak of our power, when we had an atomic monopoly, we never demanded the end of the revolution in Russia or in China. These are enormous facts. They may think we're stupid not to have made such demands, but we didn't. And even in the Korean diplomacy—I've checked very carefully with some of the people who participated in it—the nuclear threat as such was not an active part. There is a vague reference in Eisenhower's memoirs to something like a nuclear threat toward the end of the effort to achieve peace in Korea, and Secretary Acheson indicates in his book a veiled statement to the effect that the situation could well get out of hand if it weren't brought under control. But those, I think, are quite different from an ultimatum of the kind the Russians recently gave the Chinese."

"You said that under international law you can go to the aid of a government in power that's under seige, whether it's from the inside or the outside. Let's say you've got a left-wing government in South America, and there's a right-wing insurrection against it. And China—in the name of revolutionary brotherhood, balance of power, or whatever—comes to the aid of that government. How would we look at that?"

"I suppose we would face the same conundrum we faced in Cuba, with the Bay of Pigs. In that case, in the end, the power of the law in our own minds made us fall back. In George Ball's phrase—which he used at a later point, but I think it's the same idea—we would have been a different kind of country if we'd done it. In the decision-making process of Americans, there's an enormous reluctance to do that, to go against the law. There might be an occasion when we would, when we would feel that the national interest is so over-powering that we would move. But I think so far we really haven't."

"In this hypothetical situation I suggested, the Chinese would be acting in accord with international law."

"I understand. That's a tough one. Our reaction would depend on the state of tension in the world at large."

"We might break the law in the name of the Monroe Doctrine. What if they had their own Monroe Doctrine for Asia?"

"Well, but they don't," Rostow said. "And we didn't like it when the Japanese proclaimed one. I'm not try-ing to evade the question. I'm saying that the notion of law is very powerful in our psyche and that it would be difficult, but not impossible, for us to take a step in breach of international obligations."

"The way you've described our notion of security, I would think it would be harder, in this case I just sug-gested, for us *not* to break the law than to break it. It would seem fantastic for us to allow China to send troops to this hemisphere."

"Absolutely."

"Well, why can't we allow them to think it's fantastic for us to be in their back yard with five hundred thou-sand troops, or whatever the number is now?"

87

"They undertook to do that in Korea, but so far they haven't in Vietnam, and I think the reasons are clear."

"The reasons are that we're too big and powerful."

"And that we wouldn't tolerate it. Secretary Rusk said there would be no sanctuaries in this war."

"It sounds as though you're admitting that we're not willing to let them have the same concerns and worries that we have for ourselves."

"No, I'm not saying that at all," Rostow said. "I said it depends on what premise you assume Chinese policy to be working. If Chinese policy is working on the basis of national interests, we say we'll do everything in the world to respect and defer to these interests. Including withdrawal from Vietnam."

"We'll defer to those interests as long as they fit *our* definition of Chinese national interests."

"In Eastern Europe, for example, we have in effect conceded to the Soviet Union that Soviet national interests require friendly governments there. Or at least that we won't object to such governments. We've never quite swallowed it, but we don't object."

"But we haven't made a similar concession to China. We're not willing to let her have the same great-power status that we take for ourselves and grudgingly grant the Russians."

"No, I don't think that's correct, either. We've said we're not trying to undo the regime in North Korea, which is on the Chinese border. We're not trying to undo the regime in North Vietnam, which is on the

our irrational needs as well as our rational ones. But when it comes to the other side, we say, 'Well! I see no rational reason for the Russians to do this or that—it's not in their national interest.' But the definition is always ours. When we define their interests, we get to be very reasonable. When we define ours, we define the reasonable *and* the unreasonable. And then say, 'Well, that's politics, that's the way it goes.'"

"No, I think that isn't—I would come back to Eastern Europe as a very good example of a case where we said, 'Well, we can understand the Russians had these irrational concerns.'"

"Yes, I give you that one."

"And in the overriding interest of reaching an accommodation with the Russians we'll wink at this."

"Why haven't we done the same thing in Asia?"

"Haven't we? We've accepted North Vietnam, North Korea. We've accepted the takeover of China itself."

"Well, we've gone over and over that. Let me get off that for a minute. You've said that our main concern is a balance of power."

"As a step toward achieving a system of peace," Rostow said. "It has to be a reciprocal thing in the end, with mutual respect for the system as it's evolving. Or it won't last very long. And there our main hope is this enormous magnetic pull of the nuclear problem, which can be a cancerous threat and at the same time can be an enormous force driving the nuclear powers toward an accommodation."

97

"You said that our concerns were not just ideological, that we were willing to accept different social systems brought about by peaceful change rather than by aggression."

"Or violent change within a country."

"Okay. What if there were a series of changes within Asia, internal revolutions of a leftist cast, that—while they were not fomented and supported by Peking—amounted to Communist takeovers. Wouldn't the result be the creation of a bloc?"

"Absolutely."

"Which is what we don't want."

"Absolutely, and I would say we'd probably just sit by and watch it happen."

"We *would?*"

"I would think so. Just as we watched the turnover in Syria, which turned out to be very serious indeed."

"Well, then this balance would have been disturbed after all."

"Profoundly disturbed. It was disturbed by the Communist takeover in Russia and China. We've paid enormous prices for those events."

"Leaving aside the Geneva agreements and other diplomatic considerations for the moment, is there much doubt which side would have won in Vietnam if we hadn't helped one side and the Russians and Chinese hadn't helped the other?"

"Well, certainly the Communist military forces in

98

Indo-China in 1954 were stronger than any other forces there," Rostow said. "It's very likely that the Communists would have won. It's certainly a hypothesis I wouldn't want to contest. The settlement in 1954 was basically in terms of French power, with a lot of help from Vietnamese. So I suppose it's fair enough to hypothesize that if we hadn't played any part in it, the Communists might well have won. But these events didn't take place in the abstract, they happened in the setting of 1954 and our relations with France and Britain and the Philippines. You had a specter of terrific hostility and military activity in Korea, Malaysia, the Philippines, and Indo-China that were perceived at that time as a threat to national interests."

"To psychological national interests or which national interests?"

"Well, *security*. The vision of that much geography and that many people suddenly transferred—you know, the shock to American opinion of both the Bolshevik Revolution and the Communist takeover in China were very deep . . . the Red scares of the twenties . . . the McCarthy period."

"Well, we've got to quit being so shocked by the world."

"Well, no. We may have to get over being shocked by it, but these events are realities, too. There were enormous consequences to them. And we've been very quiet about shocking events in recent years. One of the striking things about the conduct of policy in recent

99

years has been the deliberate effort not to stir up hysterics. That means that shocking events take place, but we don't react to them with shock. We're very calm and rational about them, although they have the potentiality of blowing up some fine morning, if they're pushed to an extreme point."

"Still, just to get it clear in my mind, no one can imagine a real military defeat of the United States now, in the way that they perhaps could have before the Second World War, can they?"

"That all depends on the nuclear balance."

"Yes, they could shoot missiles at us, but I mean no one could occupy this country."

"You can shoot missiles at us or you can destroy the Navy."

"But I mean, as a practical matter, nobody could occupy us, could they? Occupy a country with such a big Army and so many missiles?"

"And so many hunting rifles," Rostow said. "No, but the problem of the nuclear threat is that it poses itself in a different form. That's what makes the ABM so complex. Suppose you wake up one morning and are faced with this statement: 'We have defensive missiles and you don't. We can attack you but you can't attack us. Now please get out of Europe and the Middle East.'"

"We'd be pretty skeptical about that, wouldn't we?"

"But I'm just giving that as an illustration. Because you have a proliferation of technology now, and you never know what the potential of some laser or blazer or some other miserable scientific gadget can be."

"You mean there might be a foolproof defense against all missiles?"

"I'm not at all sure. I've been to dozens of those briefings and tried my best to quiz and cross-examine the experts, and they could never give any guarantees as to where these things were going. You see, you're dealing with new technologies, new scientific methods."

"But don't they imagine heading off most of the missiles that might be fired at us?"

"Well, yes, they do now. But what's the potential for this technique five or ten years from now? We don't know. That's the problem."

"That's an imponderable that doesn't have anything to do with all of this balance-of-power business, isn't it?"

"They're linked. The role of the nuclear deterrent in this balance process is a reality."

"Yes, but in the hypothetical situation you suggested —we wake up tomorrow and Russia has created some sort of missile shield—the geographical and the manpower elements of the balance don't mean anything any more."

"The assumption, so far, is that the nuclear weapons in Soviet and American hands neutralize each other. We're trying to keep the game small enough to be predictable. If you've got deuces wild, if Nasser has nuclear weapons, you don't know where you are. It's a game nobody can play."

"Is that another part of the balance idea? We feel we

101

have to cool down disorders and make small countries feel protected, because if they don't feel protected they might get nuclear weapons. Because even if we weren't bombed we would suffer from fallout—is that part of it?"

"That's right. Not only fallout. After all, a nuclear weapon doesn't carry a flag. You don't know where it comes from."

"Yes, but what if you just had two little countries that were going to bomb each other, and the Russians and the Americans got together and said, 'Well, let them bomb each other.'"

"That happens."

"But not with nuclear weapons."

"Not so far," Rostow said. "There's always the possibility that if nuclear weapons become dispersed that somebody would try to trigger a war that he couldn't finish. He'd have that potential of firing a nuclear weapon at us or at the Soviet Union. And nobody would know where it came from."

"That could happen outside this framework of the balance of power."

"Of course it could."

"It could even be the Mafia or someone."

"Yes."

"I think Richard Rovere has written that we can foresee the time when private groups could get the bomb."

"That's why they tell me—that the technology is well

102

known, and the proliferation of power plants around the world, creating a source of uranium, could well permit such a development."

"How does the balance of power figure in that situation?"

"It doesn't. The balance game posits, assumes, that somehow or other the major powers are going to keep the nuclear weapon out of actual use and even implied use or threat, except for a very major concern. And it assumes that the nuclear club will be kept small. Whether that's going to be possible I don't know. And whether the world will be manageable under such circumstances I haven't the faintest idea. But you've got a situation now in which the protected states—Cuba, Egypt, North Vietnam, North Korea—can take very dangerous initiatives, which their protectors can't always control."

"Does Cuba have any way of manufacturing a bomb?"

"Oh, I don't know. They tell me any reasonably clever scientist can do it. But the Cubans pursue a quite independent policy so far as the Soviet Union is concerned. Their calculation is that the Soviet Union, for reasons of its own, isn't going to dare to abandon them and allow us to take over."

"Well, I guess that would be an argument in favor of your balance theory, if not of all its applications."

"It sure would."

"It might be to our advantage for some of these hostile states to be under the assumed control of Russia."

"That's right. And so long as you can assume some understanding between us and the Soviets . . . Well, that's how it's evolving."

SEVEN

Circles

"Well, that part of your explanation makes some sense to me," I said. "It's when we start trying to apply the theory to specific cases, to fighting over specific pieces of ground in Asia, that you lose me. There, I have to say again that we just keep going in circles. We talk about the balance of power only in terms of that balance. You say we have to do such-and-such in Vietnam. I say, 'Why?' You say, 'To preserve a balance of power.' I say, 'Why do we have a balance of power in Asia?' You say, 'So we can have a system of order, so we don't withdraw into a Fortress America, so we aren't left with nothing but a nuclear option, and so that we can deal with problems in a conventional diplomatic and military way.' But what problems? Problems like Vietnam and Laos. But these appear to be problems in the first place only because they're seen in terms of this balance-of-power theory. So we've come full circle. We

105

have the balance in order to deal with the problems, and we have to deal with the problems in order to preserve the balance. The theory is eating its own tail. I understand the need for the balance in Europe and the Middle East, but as far as Asia is concerned I still don't get it."

"I can see what you mean," Rostow said. "Your problem arises, I think, because you have too much faith in nuclear weapons. Well, to confine ourselves to the Asian problem for a moment—if we can separate these things, which I doubt. Let me explain that for a minute. You can see now in the Middle East that the credibility of deterrence in one place affects the credibility of deterrence in another. As I read it now, the Russians are putting the heat on President Nixon, trying to determine what kind of reactions he's capable of, in ways which desperately affect the risk of war in the Middle East. And what we do in Asia affects our credibility, because the American people have to make the same kinds of decisions about how we back our commitments in Europe, in Asia, and in the Middle East. I suppose the best way I can answer your question is to say that the notion of the balance of power, of trying to preserve some kind of equilibrium in Asia, requires us to participate in a relationship of four major countries; that is, the Soviet Union, Japan, China, and the United States. And there are two very large countries, India and Indonesia, whose fate would affect the entire political and economic, and even military—certainly stra-

106

tegic—situation in that area. And then you get the special question of Australia and New Zealand, where you would run risks that would be very emotional."

"But we're explaining the balance in terms of itself again. You say we need a balance to preserve equilibrium in Asia, and I want to know why we need equilibrium in Asia. As far as Japan is concerned, for instance—if Japan shifts to another bloc and becomes a nuclear threat, don't you reach a point of redundancy? I mean, the present nuclear power is so overwhelming on both sides that an addition wouldn't make that much difference."

"Oh, no, I don't agree with that. Under such circumstances, the nuclear equation would not remain bipolar, and deterrence would become much more difficult. For example, a nuclear power might think that it had the capacity to start a nuclear war to force our hand, or to force the Russians' hand. And that was the original British and French justification for independent nuclear power—not that such power would be an independent deterrent but that they could start a war which we would have to finish. It's not a theory we've ever enjoyed very much, and that's one of the reasons, I think, that we keep such a tight hold on NATO. The same kind of reasoning would apply to Japan. The Japanese might pursue a risky course toward China, or toward Russia, as the case might be, confident that in the end our interest in their independence would be enough to justify it. You're moving into a much more unstable and much

107

more dangerous situation as the number of nuclear powers increases. This defines the general fear of nuclear proliferation—that politics would become a card game with all the deuces wild. You wouldn't know how to control it, or you would always live in terror of something. That's why we and the Russians agreed on the nuclear-nonproliferation treaty."

"What if the Japanese were not another independent power but were allied with China? It would be just more of the same. More nuclear missiles."

"It would be very dangerous to us."

"But why is that? An alliance between Japan and China could mean more missiles to defend against—is that what you're talking about?"

"Well, or the use of nuclear threats. To make the western Pacific a Japanese lake."

"What's our concern with the western Pacific? I mean, then you get back to—"

"You get back to why we are interested in the first place," Rostow said. "Trade, movement, fear . . . a sense that these— The two big changes that have occurred, the Communist revolutions in China and Russia, have cost us an enormous amount. Trying to deter and contain their expansion. The feeling that if they expanded indefinitely, we would face a situation in which we really felt threatened all the time."

I quoted to Rostow from an article by Robert L. Heilbroner, "Counter-Revolutionary America," which appeared first in *Comemntary* and later in a paperback

collection entitled *A Dissenter's Guide to Foreign Policy.*
Heilbroner said in the article that even if much of the
underdeveloped world turned Communist and became
hostile to the United States, the resulting military threat
would be slight. We wouldn't be threatened by millions
of men who couldn't be deployed, and the armaments
capacities of these areas are small, he said. If we lost
the entire sixteen billion dollars invested in Latin America, Asia, and Africa, it would be a blow to some
corporations, he said, but—with our gross national
product approaching three-quarters of a trillion dollars
and our total corporate assets amounting to more than
one and three-tenths trillion—it would be tolerable.
Heilbroner went on to say, "By these remarks I do not
wish airily to dismiss the dangers of a Communist
avalanche in the backward nations. There would be
dangers, not the least those of an American
hysteria."

Rostow said he didn't disagree with Heilbroner's
analysis.

"About the economics and the manpower," I said.
"But you don't agree completely, because Heilbroner
says later in the article that much of the motivation for
our anti-Communism is a fear of our not being the
model for world civilization, a fear of losing our place
in the sun."

"I don't agree with that at all," Rostow said, "I don't
think our foreign policy is based on a place-in-the-sun
psychology. I don't think we get any pleasure out of

109

our position. I recall George Aiken's remark. He said we've inherited the responsibilities but not the privileges of the British Empire. I don't think any Americans enjoy it. But I think there would be a sense of strategic threat if the changes Heilbroner describes took place. In the emplacement of missiles, for example, just as there was over Cuba and there remains over Cuba. Cuba is a gnawing anxiety in the Congress, really. More than you might think. And the missiles there—we can say very rationally, 'Oh, hell, they have missiles in submarines, why should we fret over whether they have them in Cuba or not? But a threat of being surrounded—what Heilbroner calls hysteria—I don't think can be discounted. And the strategic space problems, the emplacement of bases all around, can become a major element of politics."

"We were talking about Japan before I mentioned the Heilbroner article," I said. "We speak of the pressures that Japan might put on us if she changed the direction of her policy. But our fears about her go back to the last war, and then she didn't just put pressures on us—she attacked us directly."

"Yes, but the Japanese attacked us in a context in which we were moving more and more to curb their expansion. We were becoming concerned. Not so much over Korea, more so about Manchuria, and then still more as they began to move south—threatened to move south with great force into Southeast Asia. Heilbroner calls that concern hysteria, but it's a hysteria that has

110

to be taken into account as a fact. It's a very natural reaction,and I should say a rational one."

"But at that time we could imagine their expanding throughout the Pacific, and then, with weapons being what they were at the time, actually trying to come over here and bomb us, or bring ships over to shell us, or something, couldn't we?"

"We could, but basically what the Japanese wanted was a green light in Asia, which we wouldn't give them. And we were visibly becoming more and more concerned, despite the developing threats in Europe. We were becoming equally concerned about Japanese expansion in the Pacific. So they moved on Pearl Harbor in that context."

"Well, at that time, what was our fear from Japan? Didn't it ultimately go back to—"

"Hegemony. Hegemony."

"I know. There's that word. But you've said that our fear is no longer merely one of invasion, implying that at one time that *was* a great fear. In one of your articles, you say that we used to worry about a European power's coming over and establishing a beachhead from which it could attack us or exert some influence on us."

"That was our reaction at the end of the Civil War, you see. We told Maximilian to get the hell out of Mexico. You can articulate it as a fear of invasion if you want to, but it's a fear of having any very strong power there that could be a threat to us, in a number of ways."

111

"But what I'm trying to get at is this: Isn't it true that one large consideration that existed then—the possibility of invasion—is not very feasible anymore on either side?"

"No, the nuclear weapon just doesn't make that much difference. The fear of a superior conventional power is still as real as ever, because nuclear weapons can't really be used. Did you ever read that marvellous book, *The Zimmerman Telegram,* by Barbara Tuchman? Superb. An account of the Zimmerman-telegram episode before we got into the First World War. It concerned an idea the Germans had of fooling around with the Mexicans, and the idea of a Japanese presence in Mexico was involved. We were just as sensitive to that as we were to Maximilian or to Castro. And for the same sort of reason. Rational or irrational, that's how people behave. It isn't, I suppose, that we feared that Maximilian was going to send the French Foreign Legion into Texas. We just didn't want the French there."

"What was the problem then?" I asked. "How could the French have made trouble for us?"

"I don't suppose it was ever articulated. I've never gone back and looked in any of the histories. It was just a sense that that was something we didn't want. We wanted a hegemonic position in America, we didn't want any great powers here, and that was our national interest. We had got along with the British, although we had had some troubles with them, but we were damned if we were going to see the French in Mexico.

112

Now, could it have been articulated or rationalized in any other way? I don't know."

"If we assume that invasion today is not practical and that no one would be foolish enough to try it, and assume that we did 'lose' Japan, what are some of the things the Japanese might do in the Pacific that we would find unacceptable—or that they *could* do?"

"It's exactly as you say, it's precisely like our concern about Germany in Europe in 1917 and 1940. I should suppose it would be a policy of emplacement in the southern Pacific that would be a potential interference with our own movements. Movements of trade and of people, access to the countries, political effects, and so on."

"Is that behind many of these concerns—our free movement?"

"Yes, you find that best articulated, I think, in some of Bill Fulbright's speeches. We need a world of wide horizons, we want a world of wide horizons—"

"But that's so vague. You can say those things, and they sound good, they sound reasonable, but what do they mean?"

"You mean why do we care about Cambodia?"

"Yes. I just don't understand. Is it a fear that I won't be able to move from country to country? Is it trade?"

"Trade isn't the key to it. Heilbroner's economic analysis is perfectly reasonable. The trade that counts for the United States is with Canada, Western Europe, and Japan. That's the bulk of it. And we could survive without most of that trade, I suppose. It isn't that. It's the sense of being hemmed in that becomes so dangerous. Now, you can say that that's irrational, and that we ought to get over it. To which my answer would be that this has been the major cause of war for all the centuries since Thucydides wrote."

"Of all the arguments you've advanced in support of your balance-of-power view, which do you think is the most persuasive?" I asked. "You emphasize psychological dangers, the difficulty of maintaining our way of life in a Fortress America—would these be your greatest concerns?"

"Yes," Rostow said. "I should say that the basic concern for me is the potentiality of remaining the kind of society we are at home and minimizing the risk of a war that might result from our being surrounded and threatened, politically, or otherwise. And that's where I think that if you look back at the history of the onset of any war, you see how the psychological mechanism works. In the thirties, the British and French said, 'We're not going to go to war over the Rhineland or Czechoslovakia,' but then when the crisis came in Poland they went to war, prepared or not, because they felt this hegemonic spectre. And we're not immune from that, you see. Nobody is."

"But, given someone like Hitler—we were faced with a lot more than a psychological threat from him. He wanted to take over the—"

"*Well*. Rusian policy is not benign. Russian policy is

very sinister to deal with. We don't shout about it, but it's very, very grim. You can't even work out a deal with the Russians on the Middle East. And they make a deal and then go back on it."

"Are they not any different from what they were in the days of Stalin? You read about how they're getting to be more reasonable, about how our two systems are getting to be more alike, and so on. Are they still wild-eyed revolutionaries? Do they want to take over the world?"

"I wouldn't say the world. As far as their Middle Eastern policy is concerned, I regard it as part of their policy toward Europe. Its goals are to dismantle NATO and get the fleet out of Mediterranean and neutralize Europe."

"And then do what?"

"That's for the next generation. But that's quite a lot—to isolate us completely. The shock of that I don't think we would take, and I don't think the Europeans would take it."

"If we *did* take it, how would it change our lives? Physically, without the emotion—though I realize you can't avoid the emotion."

"I should think that the ideological atmosphere in the United States would change completely," Rostow said. "Advocates of an accommodation with the Russians, and, you know, ending the arms race, and coöperating, and compromising, and agreeing to their terms, would become very much stronger—the Henry Wallace sort of

115

phenomenon. In our politics, in our internal life. Governments in Western Europe would become coalition governments, and there would be Comunist penetration, and Communist strength would become more visible. Communist orientation. And you would begin to move into exactly the kind of situation that I would fear most, in terms of our internal life. You would begin to transform the internal life here the way you would in countries that are subject to that sort of pressure. I don't mean we would become Poland, but we would begin to move toward that kind of posture."

"I thought the argument was just the reverse—that if we felt hemmed in, we would have a right-wing government that would—"

"Yes, that we would have one group of people who would say, 'We have to to get ready to nuke 'em to kingdom come and stand guard.' But that's a futile policy anyway. And you would have another group who would say, 'Well, why do that? That's foolish. Why should the world come to an end? What they propose is reasonable, after all. Let's just accommodate ourselves to them and stop being hostile to Communism.' There was quite a lot of opinion like that about Hitler, both here and in Europe."

"Wouldn't there be a large group who didn't want to go to war but wanted to have a right-wing government that would keep America pure?"

"That's correct. Therefore, we would be subjected to terrific tensions. Our society would be split apart. That's

116

one of the things I mean when I say that becoming a garrison state would make anything we could identify as democracy very problematical. I think it would be a terrible risk—the political consequences of it."

"All right," I said. "That's Europe. But I keep going back to Asia and to your fears about Japan and China. If Japan did become a nuclear power and did form an alliance with China, what would be some of the concrete things that Japan and China might do to bring pressure on us in the Pacific?"

"I'm trying not to be bound by the past, not to think about Korea and Indonesia and so on," Rostow said. "I'll resist the temptation to say the problem is very like that of Europe, although I think it is. I suppose the geography of the situation has its own logic anyway. I should suppose that what they might do is to interpose a presence that would threaten our freedom of the seas, our freedom of movement, except on political terms that we might or might not find very difficult. And to constitute a power center that could in itself be threatening. That kind of thing might—ought to, logically—force us into a much closer association with the Russians. Now, that might or might not be feasible. And if Japan joined with China, broke loose from us, in a really radical shift—"

"Yes, and if we were letting them run wild in Asia—that's what I'm asking about. We're not protecting Korea now, in this hypothetical situation, because the idea of protecting Korea was to protect Japan, and so

117

on—so all that is gone. Because there's nothing there we want. So that leaves Japan and China with the ability to become a nuclear threat to us—and to do what?"

"Well, to become a hegemonic power in Asia. You would be putting the enormous potential power of China and the naval power of Japan together in one lump, and that's just the kind of thing that has stirred the hackles of foreign-policy experts forever, because of the potentiality of harm in a great many places."

"But we're assuming, just for the moment, that there's not going to be a nuclear war. So all you're saying is that this development would mean hegemonic power in Asia, and we just can't allow that—period. But I'm trying to—"

"Discover why. I know."

"If the Asians are not going to bomb us—which, of course, you can't assume. Maybe they would."

"They did before."

"Right," I said. "But before nuclear bombs. But if you assume they wouldn't start a nuclear war—"

"But, don't forget, we bombed them with nuclear weapons."

"I know, but that wasn't the same, because there was no threat that they would bomb us back with nuclear weapons. They didn't have any. Now we're assuming that both sides are nuclear, and that there's a standoff, just as there is with the Russians."

"Well, I don't know," Rostow said. "There you get the ABM element."

118

"The defensive thing. You have to have more missiles to knock their missiles down."

"Yes, But they could probably defend Japan against the United States with ABMs."

"But say it's a stalemate."

"And then we see Japan and China working together to govern the whole of Asia," Rostow said. "Do we care? Does it make any difference to us in any fundamental sense?"

"Right," I said. "If we're not protecting Japan, why are we worried about Burma and Malaysia and Korea and all that? And, of course, I agree that the nuclear business is not to be sneezed at, but I'm assuming nuclear stalemate and then trying to find out if, in conventional ways, it would make much difference to us."

"I should think the only answer would be that such a constellation of power could make a great deal of conventional trouble, of the kind that people have known in the past from expansionist powers," Rostow said. "That is, the expansionist disease gets going and it gets out of control. Bismarck was very restrained compared to the Kaiser. But when these fellows have got into the mood of expansion, from the time of Gustavus Adolphus, they've always gone off and expanded."

"So where might the Japanese expand if they were in that mood?"

"Presumably, the most rational place to expand without provoking an instant reaction from us would be south, as they did before. And there the risk would be

119

the same kind that motivated F.D.R. when he began to get more and more alarmed about Indo-China and Indonesia. And, with the ultimate threat to Australia, would we sit by and take that from the Japanese? The best argument for that that I've been able to make, and a much better one than any of the anti-Vietnam people have made, is that, having swallowed a camel in China, why should we strain at a gnat in Vietnam? But Indonesia is a very important place strategically, from the point of view of air power and sea power."

"Why?"

"Just where it is. A system of airbases radiating out from there would control a very large part of the Pacific. Now, you can say, 'What the hell do we care about the Pacific?' but we always *have* cared."

"Yes, that's what I say. What the hell do we care? If it isn't a matter of trade and money, some Marxist explanation, then—"

"Then why should we care? The threat is just as great from Japan as it would be from Japan plus Indonesia?"

"Yes."

"If you're talking about nuclear threats."

"Right."

"But, you see," Rostow said, "the problem is that if you assume a nuclear stalemate, then you have to talk about conventional threats of air power and sea power and the control of access to areas, and the threat of political control over areas. If you do that—that is, escape from the nuclear problem—then you are back in the grooves of human history. And the only system of peace that has worked at all for any period of time, except for that of the Romans, of course, is the balance of power of the nineteenth century."

"I can see why we want access to Europe but I'm still confused about why we want access to anything in Asia, once you give up Japan. Your explanations have told me things I didn't know about ways of trying to hold on to Japan, but if we did let her go, and had a nuclear stalemate, I can't see what would follow from that."

"I suppose your scenario might be conceivable, if tense, until you got an issue like Australia or Israel, which would stir you up beyond control. If you said, 'Oh, hell, we'll wash our hands of Japan, we'll wash our hands of the major power base in Asia and let that go loose and find its own level,' then I suppose it would follow, just like my argument about Vietnam, that if you swallowed a camel, why strain at a gnat? But Indonesia strikes me as— Maybe this is just bad education, thinking in naval terms, but Indonesia strikes me as a very significant place, in terms of trying to maintain any sense of control over your whole political and strategic position in the Pacific."

"If you're *in* there," I said. "If you're in the Pacific, you have to protect your presence. But I'm trying to get us out, so that we don't have anything to protect, and to ask what the consequences of that would be."

"Well, we've got Hawaii, of course."

"Well, *sure*. The Asian powers might fool with you on

121

a little nibble here and there, but I'm assuming they wouldn't try anything with Hawaii. They might as well attack the mainland. So if we don't have any real trade needs in the Pacific, I still don't get it."

"I suppose the most *nearly* rational answer would be —and I'm not sure you're dealing with rationality here— that the formation of foreign policy has always been addressed, for reasons that make a lot of sense, to potentialities," Rostow said. "Trying to prevent potential threats from developing. For centuries, the British tried to prevent any one power from dominating Europe in a way that could totally threaten the U.K. The world is much smaller than it was before 1914, especially with the air-power dimensions, to say nothing of the nuclear dimensions. I think that what we're talking about is two different concepts of safety. You're saying that as long as we're not subject to invasion—and presumably we can have enough air power in the continental United States to make the idea of a naval invasion of this country very expensive—and as long as we keep a nuclear stalemate, then the hell with everything. It wouldn't make any difference. Europe, Japan—"

"I'm not really saying that. I'm keeping Europe and saying the hell with Asia."

"But logically, can you do that? You wouldn't see a possible combination of Japan and China or Japan and Russia as a threat to any interest in Asia that we should regard as important?"

"No, I wouldn't, not knowing anything about it. I

122

don't know what our interests there *are*. You say we have to protect our interests to preserve the balance, and we have to have the balance to protect our interests. It depends on what you mean by interests. I just don't see how we can be much more threatened than we already are. And it looks as if we get into trouble by exposing ourselves to it in the name of this balance theory, and as if the theory is just eating its tail. It's a circular kind of—"

"But you say you agree about Europe, you agree about Japan."

"No, I don't agree about Japan. If you told me our economy was going to collapse if we couldn't trade in the Pacific and in Asia, then that would be different. I'd go along with you. But you won't give me that to hang on to."

"I won't, no," Rostow said. "We could probably adjust to damn near anything economically, if we set our minds to it. We don't depend very much on external trade, and never have. Sure, we have an enormous agricultural-export industry, but it's much more other people needing our exports than anything else. Yes, you'd have to change—cut back farm acreage, all that sort of thing. But I wouldn't say that the American economic problem is insuperable without foreign trade, because I don't think it is. I think that political security requires this degree of prevention of control. And I say that by conceding the importance of Europe for the reasons you give, you simply confirm my whole argument. Now, you

123

ask me to be particular about what could happen if these changes came about in Asia, and I can't be. You say the theory eats its tail. Well, in a sense you're right. All I can say is that, in terms of human history, it has always been very dangerous for people when a potentially hostile power establishes hegemony. I can't particularize how that potential hostility would be exercised, but I would prefer, even at considerable cost, to prevent the risk. Now, you can say that that's the theory eating its tail—you start from a premise and you prove that the application of the premise leads to certain very expensive and unpleasant things. That's right. The question is: Is the premise sensible?"

"Right. That's what the whole discussion is about."

"Either the premise is sensible as a way of minimizing the risk of general war or it isn't. Can I demonstrate that catastrophe would fall upon us if we walked out of Vietnam tomorrow? I can't. I believe that there would be a very grave risk of a change in Japanese policy. But I can't prove that to you. As for what might happen if some of these spectres actually came into existence, the only way I can particularize about them is to fall back on the past and to say this is how troubles have always developed when you had a hegemonic power interested in expansion."

"I understand that. But I'm asking if the people who manage our foreign affairs ever examine these premises and argue about them instead of just falling back on them. Isn't that worthwhile now, with the stakes so

124

high, and considering the likelihood that there will be a lot of change and turmoil in the world?"

"I completely agree with you."

"But is it being done? Do they examine these premises, or are they just too busy taking care of the daily problems, which they handle in the context that I'm trying to get outside of?"

"I'm entirely in favor of your effort," Rostow said. "I examine them all the time myself. Dean Rusk used to press our planners to do the same, and he sat with them for hours examining alternatives. I don't know what's happening now. But I'd say this about it: Nobody had a greater stake than Nixon in finding an alternative policy in Vietnam. Nothing would have done him more good at home politically, nothing could have helped the future of the Republican Party more. I think the fact that he and Kissinger and everybody else couldn't do it, that they came up with exactly the same balance-of-power analysis and the same conclusions, is very significant. Yes, I think there was a terrific reëxamination."

"But I'm just wondering if this reëxamination didn't stay within the bounds of this general theory, these premises."

"No, I don't think so. I've got enough reflections back from talks various friends have had with Henry Kissinger to indicate that the reëxamination went very far—involving all of Henry's friends at Harvard, and so on. And that alternative premises were deeply considered. Now, if, with that stake in an alternative, Nixon decided

125

that he couldn't find one, you've got to conclude at least that these ideas have a fearful grip on people."

"I'll grant you that. The grip."

"And maybe an entirely unjustified grip," Rostow said. "The only defense I can make for them is that they're tragically verified by history."

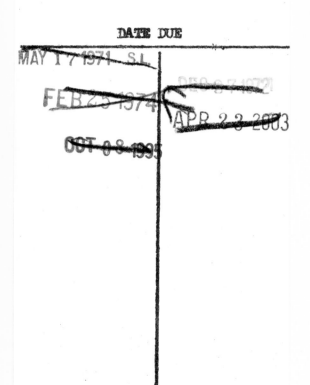